iPhone
Guide

Introduction

 iPhones are everywhere. You'll find them in people's pockets, next to their beds, clutched in their hands, falling into toilet bowls.... you get the idea. To date, Apple has sold more than a billion iPhones, which means there are twice as many iPhones in the world than pigeons (it's true - Google it).

What I'm getting at, is that a lot of people know how to use the iPhone. Most children know how to use an iPhone. They understand it with an inherent nature that's almost baffling to many adults. Maybe it's because a touchscreen makes more logical sense than a keyboard or mouse. With a touchscreen, you can just reach out and touch whatever you want to interact with.

Of course, there's much more to iPhone than just a touchscreen. It's possibly the most advanced piece of technology created by man, with components designed at the nanometer scale, and with software that can learn your routine, habits, and interests. That's what this book is all about. It's about revealing the features and abilities of the iPhone, but in a *human* way. You won't find any technical mumbo-jumbo, nor will it ramble on about features that most users don't need to know about. Instead, it will reveal the basics of the iPhone, like what it's hardware does, how it's built-in apps work, and how you can use an iPhone to enrich and improve your life. It will also include some short, snippy, humorous tips now and then, just to liven things up.

Just before I go, if there's anything you would like to know that isn't covered in this book, send me an email at tom@tapguides.co.uk, and I'll be happy to help :)

Tom Rudderham, Author

About the author

Tom Rudderham is the author of iPad Pro Guide, iPhone XS Guide, MacBook Pro Guide, Photos: the Ultimate Guide to iPhone & iPad Photography, iPad: Interactive Guide, and much more.

Tom kicked off his writing career at Future Publishing, working for magazines including MacFormat, Computer Arts, Imagine FX, and the Official Windows Magazine. Later, he became a User Experience and Interface Designer, researching, planning, and designing websites and apps for companies including Siemens, Waitrose, the IOPC, Amigo Loans, and Microsoft.

Since 2012, he has written a large range of best-selling technology books and manuals, covering every major Apple product since the launch of the iPhone 5.

Copyright © 2019 by Tap Guides Ltd
All rights reserved. No part of this publication may be reproduced, stored or transmitted in any form or by any means, electronic, mechanical, photocopying, recording, scanning, or otherwise without written permission from the publisher. It is illegal to copy this book, post it to a website, or distribute it by any other means without permission.

Published by:
Tap Guides Ltd. Exeter, EX4 5EJ

ISBN:
9781798042830

Contents

Welcome

Terminology	8
A brief history of the iPhone	10
iPhone X	18
iPhone XS & XS Max	20
iPhone XR	22
iPhone 11 Pro	24
iPhone 11	32
Pro, or no go Pro?	34
Wondering which iPhone to get?	36
Cases and screen protectors	38

The Basics

Setup and activate your iPhone	42
Face ID	44
The Lock Screen	46
The Home Screen	47
Gestures and Buttons	48
Connect to a Wi-Fi network	50
iCloud	51
How to use Control Center	52
Display Settings	54
Toggle Dark Mode	56
How to use Spotlight	58
How to manage Notifications	60
Talk to Siri	62
Accounts, emails, and passwords	64
Type like a Pro	66
How to cut, copy and paste	68
How to use the Share sheet	70
Use AirDrop to share files	71
Data Roaming & Personal Hotspots	72
Use Handoff to work between devices	74
Emergency SOS	75
Use Apple Pay to buy things	76
Use AirPlay to stream content to a TV	78

Web & Communication

Use Safari to browse the web	82
Chat using Messages	86
Check your email	96
Phone tips	100
Make a FaceTime video call	102

Camera & Photos

Take a photo using iPhone X, XR or XS	106
Take a photo using iPhone 11 or 11 Pro	114
View and edit your Photos	122

Apps, Music, & Videos

Install and manage apps	134
Listen to Music	136
Watch TV & Movies	140

Maps, News, & Utilities

Use Maps to navigate the world	144
Get the latest news	148
Monitor the stock market	150
Create Reminders	152
Create your own Siri Shortcuts	154
Create, edit, and share Notes	156
Manage your Files	160

Settings

An overview of the Settings app	164
Use Screen Time to set limits	166
How to look after your battery	168
How to use Do Not Disturb	170
A guide to Accessibility settings	172
Audio Settings	176

Troubleshooting

The Genius Bar	180
AppleCare+	182
How to erase and restore an iPhone	183
What happens to a water damaged iPhone	184
Cracked Screen	185
What to do if you lose your iPhone	186
Other Problems	187

Welcome

Since its introduction in 2007, the iPhone has changed the way we communicate, navigate, and interact with the world around us. More than ten years later, iPhone 11 and the iPhone 11 Pro continue the journey, with better cameras, longer battery life, and much more...

Contents:

Terminology	8
A brief history of the iPhone	10
iPhone X	18
iPhone XS & XS Max	20
iPhone XR	22
iPhone 11 Pro	24
iPhone 11	32
Pro, or no go Pro?	34
Wondering which iPhone to get?	36
Cases and screen protectors	38

Welcome

Terminology

Wondering what all those words and phrases mean?

The iPhone is a rather complicated piece of equipment, so perhaps it's inevitable that talking about it involves using a wide-ranging assortment of words, phrases, and terminology. In this book, you're going to hear a lot about the iPhone hardware, software, and features. Don't worry, each one of them will be explained as we go, so you'll never feel confused or get lost halfway through a paragraph. To get you started, here are a few of the words we will be using constantly throughout this book...

Whenever the word hardware is used, we're basically talking about the iPhone in its physical form. The thing which you hold in your hand.

Think of software as a set of instructions for doing something on your iPhone. These instructions might be millions of words long, and they were probably written by a large team of people. To most humans, it's utter gibberish. It looks something like this:

```
int main(int argc, char * argv[]) {
    @autoreleasepool {
        return UIApplicationMain( argc, argv, nil,
NSStringFromClass( [AVCamAppDelegate class]
) );
    }
```

To a programmer who writes in Swift (Apple's programming language), this makes perfect sense. It's just a fraction of the code required to tell your iPhone how to capture an image using its camera. The full piece of code is tens of thousands of lines long.

The word app is short for application. An application is a piece of software, separate from iOS, which lets you do something. There's an app on your iPhone for taking a picture. There's an app for sending messages. There's an app for looking at your photos. I'm sure you get the idea.

Chapter 1

iOS

This is the name of the software which powers your iPhone. It's one of the most complicated pieces of software ever created by man. It tells your iPhone how to turn on, how to take a photo, how to browse the internet, how to scan your face when you want to unlock your phone, plus so much more. It can also learn over time. iOS will learn about your habits, how you type to individual people, where you travel, what you look like and what you sound like. It uses all of this learning to help you type quicker, find photos quicker, and basically use your iPhone in a more efficient manner.

You don't have to worry about security either, because all of this personal information is fully encrypted, and the really important stuff, like your voice and face information, never leaves your phone.

When most people think of the word iOS, they imagine the home screen of their iPhone. The place where all the icons are which let you open the internet browser or email application. You can think of it like that too, but really, it's so much more.

Third-party apps

These are apps created by companies other than Apple. There are literately millions of them, and each app serves its own purpose. The most common apps you'll find include Facebook, Instagram, Amazon, and Netflix, but you can also find apps which let you add silly graphics onto photos, access your bank account, play games, and more. You'll find all of these apps in the...

App Store

Think of the App Store as a market for apps. Some apps are free, others cost a few dollars/pounds/euros. Some apps look like they are free, but ask for a payment to do something (this is called an "In-App Purchase"). You can find the App Store on your iPhone. It has a bright blue icon with an abstract "A" in the middle.

Encryption

Think of encryption as a padlock for words, but instead of 0-9 on the padlock, it's A-Z, plus 0-9. The software on your iPhone uses encryption all the time. Whenever you send a message to a friend, all the letters you type are scrambled up, sent to the other person, then de-scrambled on their phone. The same goes for video calls you make using FaceTime, your credit cards details when you check out on the internet, and much more. Nearly everything you do on your iPhone is encrypted, which is why even the FBI can't access your phone without your password or biometric information.

iCloud

Think of iCloud as a computer somewhere in the world where your photos, messages, apps, and settings are stored. Your iPhone talks to this computer over the internet everyday to backup new photos, send new messages, and check for updates.

Welcome

A brief history of the iPhone

A look at how far we've come...

You might think of the iPhone as a new gadget. One that hasn't been around for long, but it's actually been on sale for more than 11 years at the time of writing. During those 11 years, the iPhone has transformed how people interact with technology, each other, and the world around them. It's now possible to purchase products while sitting on the toilet, order a taxi without speaking to anyone, video call someone from the beach... the possibilities are endless.

Let's step back more than a decade, and take a quick look at this history of the iPhone, from it's first unveiling to the latest Product RED-colored iteration...

2007
iPhone

The world was a different place in 2007. The mobile industry was dominated by Nokia and Blackberry, while technology pundits were predicting Microsoft to be the dominant force in the years to come. Most people used their mobiles to call and text friends and family. A few took low-resolution photos. Even fewer used their phone to browse the web.

Looking back a decade later, it's obvious that 2007 was the year when the internet changed forever. It was when Twitter and Facebook began to take off, when AirBnB was dreamed up, when YouTube became truly massive. It was also the year that the iPhone was launched.

At the time, many were confused by the iPhone. They saw it as too expensive, they saw the lack of a removable battery as a backward step; and they thought the Multi-Touch keyboard was a terrible idea.

They were all missing the bigger picture, because the iPhone was the first truly handheld computer, and it made the web accessible from anywhere in the world, at any time, and in any situation. It was the moment when people became truly connected to one another, no matter where they were; and it all started with these famous words across the page...

Chapter 1

> "...a widescreen iPod with touch controls, a revolutionary mobile phone and a breakthrough internet communications device. An iPod... a phone... and an internet communicator. An iPod, a phone... are you getting it? These are not three separate devices. This is one device! And we are calling it: iPhone. Today, Apple is going to reinvent the phone."

Those words were spoken by Steve Jobs as he announced the iPhone to the world. The audience went wild. They whooped and hollered for a product they hadn't even seen yet.

Over the next hour, Steve demoed the iPhone to a captivated crowd. No one had ever seen Multi-Touch before or even thought about the idea of scrolling through lists with a finger. By the end of that morning, Apple had completely revolutionized the entire mobile phone industry. Its rivals were left in disbelief, and in public, they scrambled to play down its significance. Mike Lazaridis, CEO of Blackberry at the time said:

> *"Try typing a web key on a touchscreen on an Apple iPhone, that's a real challenge; you cannot see what you type."*

Microsoft CEO, Steve Balmer, laughed on camera while remarking:

> *"Five hundred dollars fully subsidized with a plan! I said that is the most expensive phone in the world and it doesn't appeal to business customers because it doesn't have a keyboard, which makes it not a very good email machine."*

In hindsight, these comments seem absurd, but at the time they were real concerns. Nevertheless, during the course of 2007 more than 1.4 million iPhones were sold around the world, kicking off a revolution that changed the world.

A brief history of the iPhone

2008
iPhone 3G

This was a year that kicked off a chain of events that ruined lives for millions of people. Thankfully we're not talking about a new iPhone. We're talking about the Stock Market crash, which led to a global recession that seemed to last an eon.

As this series of terrible events began to unfurl, the iPhone 3G was announced at WWDC on June 9th. It was twice as fast as the earlier model and half the price. It featured the same 3.5-inch screen, but received a significant update to its wireless radio: support for 3G UMTS, and it also came with a plastic shell that felt warmer in the hand. Just as important were the software updates: the iPhone 3G would launch alongside the App Store, enabling users to install third-party apps; MobileMe was introduced, which synced emails, calendars, and contacts across devices, and there was the introduction of Street View to the Maps app.
Maybe 2008 wasn't so bad after all.

2009
iPhone 3GS

It was the year that Barack Obama was inaugurated as the 44th President of the United States. It was also the year that the iPhone 3GS was revealed, which sported an even faster processor, 3-megapixel camera with video recording capabilities, digital compass, and support for 7.2 Mbit/s HSDPA downloading.

Alongside improved internal hardware, the iPhone 3GS was released with iPhone OS 3, which included a long-awaited copy and paste function, spotlight for searching content on the device, MMS for sending photos and video clips via the Messages app, and Push Notifications for alerting the user when new emails, tweets, and messages arrived.

2009 was also the year that the iPhone was refreshed without a radically new hardware design. This process of design evolution, instead of revolution, continues to this day with an "S" release every two years.

Chapter 1

2010
iPhone 4

As the SpaceX Dragon Capsule returned to Earth on December 9th 2010, the world watched it happen live via a crystal clear video, thanks to the Retina Display on their new iPhone 4. This pin-sharp screen packed 326 pixels into every inch of the screen, giving text the same sharpness as traditional printed text, and making images and video look more lifelike than ever before. We now take ultra-sharp mobile screens for granted, but at the time it was revolutionary.

Other new features included with the iPhone 4 were its 5 megapixel camera that recorded 720p HD video; the A4 chip for improved graphics capability; and a front-facing camera for making FaceTime calls; and while the iPhone 4 was similar in size to its predecessor, it came with a stunning new design: an uninsulated stainless steel frame sandwiched between two plates of glass. Customers instantly fell in love with it, and by the end of 2010, 47 million units had been sold.

2011
iPhone 4S

As Game of Thrones fans recovered from the shock of the first season's finale, the iPhone 4S was unleashed upon the world.

As with the iPhone 3GS, the 4s looked remarkably similar in design to its predecessor, but alongside a re-designed antenna that improved signal strength, it also included the A5 chipset; an 8-megapixel camera with support for 1080p video recording; and iOS 5, which introduced iCloud, iMessage, Notification Center and Siri.

The press heaped praise on the new device. The Verge's Joshua Topolsky stated that "...*if this were to be a car, it would be a Mercedes*" and finished by saying "Is *this the best phone ever made? That's debatable. But I can tell you this: the iPhone 4S is pretty damn cool.*"

A brief history of the iPhone

2012
iPhone 5

This was the year that saw the Tesla Model S go into production; an electric vehicle that has upended the car industry, is years ahead of the competition when it comes to software and cloud technology, and has proved that electric power is the way forward. In many ways, it's the iPhone of the automobile world.

The same year on September 12th, iPhone 5 was announced. It featured a brand new design with an aluminum-composite frame, it was 18% thinner than the iPhone 4s, 20% lighter, and had 12% less overall volume. Inside it featured the A6 chip, a 1.3GHz dual-core processor and 1GB of RAM. It debuted with iOS 6, which introduced an entirely new Maps app, the Passbook app, Siri enhancements, and Facebook integration.

Pre-orders for the iPhone 5 went live on September 14th, 2012. Within 24 hours, more than two million orders had been received. When the device finally went on sale September 21st, the total number of pre-orders was more than 20 times of the iPhone 4s. Press reviews were favorable, with Tim Stevens from Engadget stating "*This is a hallmark of design. This is the one you've been waiting for...*" and The Verge's Joshua Topolsky declaring "*...for the mass market, it's the best smartphone, period.*"

2013
iPhone 5S & 5C

This was the year that twerking became a thing. Also, China landed a rover vehicle on the Moon. It was also the year that Apple launched two new iPhones: the iPhone 5S and the iPhone 5C.

As with each "s" iteration of the iPhone, the 5S retained the familiar look of the iPhone 5, with the only significant visual change being a new gold color option. Look a little closer, however, and there was one other subtle external change: the Touch ID fingerprint sensor. This new feature enabled the iPhone 5S to recognize fingerprints, allowing the device to be unlocked with a touch of a finger, or to authorize purchases from the App Store and iTunes store without entering a password. Internally, the iPhone 5S featured the 64-bit A7 processor, which was twice as fast as the previous generation, and the rear camera included a new 5-element lens with a f/2.2 aperture that was 15% larger than before. It also had a dual-LED flash that captured better skin tones and more accurate colors.

The iPhone 5C was just as interesting. It was the first iPhone since the 3G to come in an all-plastic enclosure, and it came in five colors: green, blue, yellow, pink, and white. It didn't include the Touch ID sensor, and it was lower powered when compared to the 5S, but it came at a more affordable price, and proved to be a massive hit with the public.

Chapter 1

2014
iPhone 6 & 6 Plus

It seemed like the long-promised gaming revolution known as virtual reality was about to be realized in 2014, when the Oculus Rift developer kit unit became available to buy. It ushered in a new, immersive world of gaming that brought worlds to life like never before, but it was also buggy and plagued by a low-resolution screen.

Thankfully, the iPhone 6 came with a pin-sharp Retina Display that was .7-inches larger than earlier models, while it's bigger brother, the iPhone 6 Plus, stunned the world with a massive 5.5-inch screen.

Alongside the larger displays, the iPhone 6 and 6 Plus featured a radical overhaul to its design. For the first time, the screen curved at the edges to seamlessly meet the metal surface that covered the back, making it more comfortable to hold. It was also thinner than any iPhone to date, yet packed more power and included a longer battery life.

Internally, the iPhone 6 had plenty of new features to offer. Its all-new barometer chip sensed the air pressure to work out your relative elevation. That meant it could now track how many flights of stairs you had climbed, or the height of the hill you were walking, ensuring fitness apps could accurately work out how many calories you had burned during the day. It's upgraded 8-megapixel camera was larger than ever, with 1.5-micron-sized pixels and a $f/2.2$ aperture, while the front-facing camera captured 81% more light and could take up to 10 photos a second. Both iPhone 6 and iPhone 6 Plus could now record 1080p high-definition video at 60 frames-per-second, making action shots look more lifelike and cinematic. Both iPhones featured better battery life than previous models, with 16 days of standby time, 80 hours of audio playback and 12 hours of 3G browsing. All these new features ensured iPhone 6 and iPhone 6 Plus were the best iPhones to date.

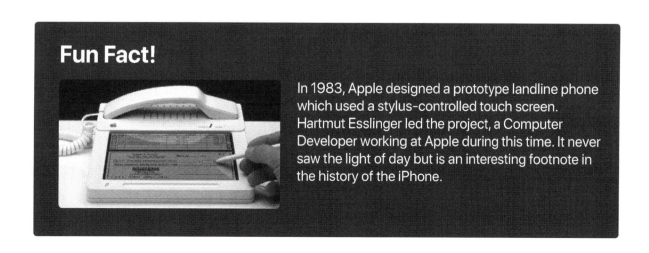

Fun Fact!

In 1983, Apple designed a prototype landline phone which used a stylus-controlled touch screen. Hartmut Esslinger led the project, a Computer Developer working at Apple during this time. It never saw the light of day but is an interesting footnote in the history of the iPhone.

A brief history of the iPhone

2015
iPhone 6S

This was the year that tech started to become really interesting. Tesla rolled out the first version of Autopilot, private space companies began reusing rockets, live streaming became a thing, Instagram became bigger than Twitter, and on September 9th, the iPhone 6S was announced.

On first appearances there's wasn't much to differentiate iPhone 6S from the iPhone 6. It was a hair thicker, 11% heavier and came in a rose gold color, but when investigated deeper it turned out that everything internally had changed or been upgraded from the previous model.

For the first time since the launch of the original iPhone, iPhone 6S introduced a new way to interact with apps and iOS: 3D Touch. It worked by detecting how much pressure was applied to the display, and offered two new Multi-Touch gestures: Peek and Pop. Peek was enabled by pressing lightly on an app, message, link or photo, and offered a sneak preview of the content within; while Pop was enabled by pressing firmly, and instantly took the user to the relevant content. In addition to 3D Touch, iPhone 6S also responded with subtle taps and bumps, letting users feel a press on the screen.

iPhone 6S included not one, but two brand new cameras which improved the clarity and color of photos. The back-facing camera was upgraded from 8 to 12-megapixels, which meant a 50% increase in detail. To ensure these higher-resolution photos looked as beautiful as ever, iPhone 6S included a new image signal processor, advanced pixel technology, Focus Pixels and improved local tone mapping, all of which meant every photo captured looked beautiful and in focus.

In additional to sharper images, iPhone 6S also captured Live Photos. These were brief moments in time, captured just before and after the camera shutter button was pressed, and they were brought to life as short video segments when the user pressed firmly on the photo.

Alongside improvements to image quality, iPhone 6S could record 4K video footage. That's cinema quality in detail, and four times higher than HD video. On the front of iPhone 6S, the FaceTime HD camera was upgraded to 5-megapixels in quality, which meant selfies looked better than ever before. In addition to the upgraded FaceTime HD camera, the Retina HD display now acted as a camera flash, illuminating 3 times brighter than usual for just a brief second when a photo was captured in the dark.

Every year the iPhone achieves new levels of performance and efficiency with an upgraded CPU and GPU, and the iPhone 6S was no different with the A9 chip. It was a 64-bit desktop-class processor that was 70% faster than the previous generation and with a graphics performance boost of a staggering 90%. The M9 chip connected to the accelerometer, compass, gyroscope, and barometer to monitor daily fitness, activity, and movements. It also listened for voice prompts at all times, enabling the user to say "Hey Siri" out-loud and immediately activate Siri.

Chapter 1

2016
iPhone 7

As two countries across the Atlantic ocean went to the polls to decide their future, the iPhone 7 was revealed to the world on 7th September 2016. It looked similar to its predecessor, with the same size screen and hardware, but the iPhone 7 and 7 Plus packed a new camera system, stereo speakers, better battery life, a brighter and more colorful display, and a more powerful CPU. Two new finishes were are also introduced: matte black and Jet Black, the latter with a polished evocative look that's utterly beautiful to behold.

For the first time, all iPhone 7 models included optical image stabilization, which helped to reduce motion blur, particularly in low-light conditions. An improved $f/1.8$ aperture allowed up to 50 percent more light into the lens, and a quad-LED True Tone flash was 50 percent brighter than the iPhone 6s. On the front of iPhone 7 was a brand new 7MP camera, enabling sharper and more vibrant selfies. Perhaps the biggest improvement to the camera system was on the iPhone 7 Plus, which now included two camera lenses on the back of the device; one with a fixed wide-angle lens and the other with a 2x zoom telephoto lens.

Other improvements to the iPhone 7 included a new Taptic Engine chip, IP67 waterproofing, and a wide color gamut display. The iPhone 7 also dropped support for wired headphones, which coincided with the release of the Apple AirPods; an amazing pair of wireless headphones with an innovative charging case.

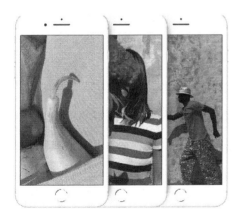

2017
iPhone 8

The iPhone 8 and 8 Plus might look similar to the iPhone 7, but every element of its hardware was improved to make it a more beautiful and powerful device. Externally, the iPhone 8 came in three new finishes: space grey, silver, and gold, and it had the most durable glass ever in a smartphone, wrapped by a laser-welded, aerospace-grade aluminum band.

The display of iPhone 8 and 8 Plus introduced True Tone technology, which adjusted the white balance of the screen to match the surrounding environment, making images look more natural and vibrant. To ensure music, calls and video sounded better than before, the iPhone 8 featured a redesigned stereo system that was 25% louder than the iPhone 7. iPhone 8 continued to support Touch ID, enabling users to unlock the phone with just a fingertip. The use of the Home button for Touch ID ensured the device looked remarkably similar to previous devices, while keeping the same screen-to-device ratio. Other improvements included the A11 Bionic chip, dual 12MP cameras, and wireless charging, all of which were shared with the iPhone X; released alongside the iPhone 8.

A brief history of the iPhone

2017
iPhone X

The iPhone X was the most significant leap forward since the original iPhone, and promised to set the course for the next ten years of smartphone development.

Like the iPhone 8, it had glass on both the front and back of the device, with a stainless steel band that wrapped around the middle. It was water and dust resistant and came in two finishes; space grey and silver. It also had an all-new display, called the Super Retina Display. At 5.8-inches in sizes and with a 2436x1125 resolution, it was the highest pixel density display ever shipped with an iPhone.

The iPhone X was the first device from Apple to include an OLED screen with full suport for HDR playback; and like the iPhone 8, it also included True Tone technology, which adjusted the white balance of the screen to match the ambience around the device.

The iPhone X was perhaps most recognizable by a small notch which ran along the top of the display. So recognizable was this notch that rival phone manufacturers quickly began to copy the design, releasing phones with the same notch, but with minor changes to avoid any copyright infringements. The notch on iPhone X housed some of the most sophisticated technology ever developed for an iPhone:

- Ambient light sensor
- Speaker
- Proximity Sensor
- Flood Illuminator
- Microphone
- 7MP camera
- Infrared Camera
- Dot Projector

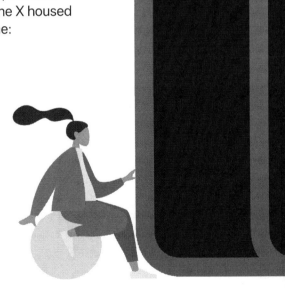

Called the TrueDepth Camera System, these combined technologies enabled the iPhone X to recognize your face, play audio, and enable you to make video calls.

Other new features exclusive to the iPhone X included new gestures to replace the Home button, a taller screen (12-13% additional screen area, when compared to earlier 4.7" iPhones), and cameras orientated vertically on the back, instead of horizontally.

Chapter 1

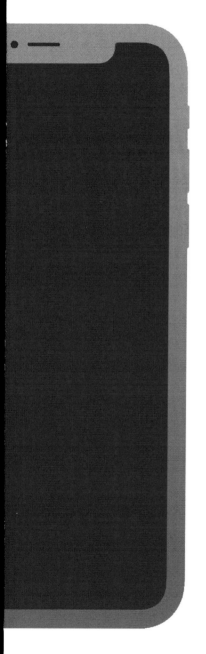

Tech Specs

Internals:
Screen: 5.8" 2436 x 1125 OLED
Processor: A11 Bionic
RAM: 3GB
Cameras: 12MP rear, 7MP front
Battery: 2716mAh
Storage: 64 / 256GB

Dimensions:
Height: 5.65"
Width: 2.79"
Thickness: 7.77mm
Weight: 174 grams

Extra vertical screen space

The width of the iPhone X matches that of the 4.7" displays on iPhone 6, iPhone 7 and iPhone 8, but it's 145 points taller, giving an extra 20% vertical space for content. Here's a diagram to help better explain:

It's worth noting that a small chunk of that 20% extra vertical space is taken up the notch. Do some mathematics to eliminate that notch and you actually get 12-13% additional screen area, when compared to earlier 4.7" iPhones.

Welcome

2018
iPhone XS & XS Max

The ultimate iPhone...

Every odd year, the iPhone received an "S" update. Think of it as a spec bump. The design stays the same, but everything inside gets refreshed and upgraded with better specifications. In short, they get faster, the cameras get better, and the hardware is refined even more. 2018 was no different, as it saw the release of both the iPhone XS and the iPhone XS Max.

Before we go any further, it's worth noting that the iPhone XS is pronounced "*iPhone ten s*", not "*iPhone excess*". Same goes for the Max, it's "*iPhone ten s max*", not "*iPhone excess max*". It's an easy mistake to make.

As you might expect, the iPhone XS was the most advanced iPhone Apple ever created for its time. It was made form a surgical-grade stainless steel, it had a gold finish on the front and back, it had better cameras, and of course, there was a bigger version to choose from: the iPhone XS Max.

iPhone XS came in three colors: gold, silver, and space grey. The phones were protected from dust and liquids to an IP68 rating, which meant you could drop your iPhone into a liquid of two meters deep, for up to 30-minutes, and not see any damage to the internal components. That included most types of liquid too. The iPhone XS was tested in clean water, seawater, chlorinated water, tea, and even beer.

Like the iPhone X, the displays on both the iPhone XS and XS Max supported full HDR playback, so you could watch movies such as LEGO Batman in Dolby Vision. Similarly, any photos you took using the iPhone XS looked incredibly realistic when viewed back on its screen.

Chapter 1

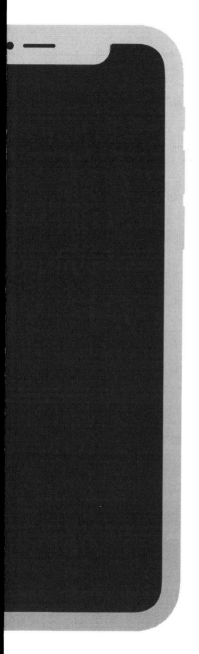

> **Tech Specs**
>
> **Internals:**
> XS Screen: 5.8" 2436x1125 OLED
> XS Max Screen: 6.5" 2688x1242 OLED
> Processor: A12 Bionic
> XS RAM: 3GB
> XS Max RAM: 3GB / 4GB
> Cameras: Dual 12MP rear, 7MP front
> XS Battery: 2,658mAh
> XS Max Battery: 3,174mAh
> Storage: 64 / 256 / 512GB
>
> **iPhone XS Dimensions:**
> Height: 5.65"
> Width: 2.79"
> Thickness: 7.7mm
> Weight: 174 grams
>
> **iPhone XS Max Dimensions:**
> Height: 6.2"
> Width: 3.05"
> Thickness: 7.7mm
> Weight: 208 grams

Screen sizes

The iPhone XS came in two sizes: one with a 5.8-inch display, and another with a 6.5-inch display. This latter model had the biggest display ever shipped on an iPhone. Here's a quick image comparing both iPhone XS and iPhone XS Max with the iPhone 8 Plus:

Welcome

2018
iPhone XR

Color to the max...

When it shipped September 2018, the iPhone XR had the largest LCD display ever shipped in an iPhone. It also had the same camera lens included with the iPhone XS, and the same A12 Bionic chip, making it an incredible piece of technology for its price point. It's also came in six bold color choices: white, black, blue, coral, yellow, and (PRODUCT)RED™.

The iPhone XR was an incredibly interesting device. It arrived onto the market just one month after the iPhone XS and XS Max. Two devices that cost hundreds of dollars more to purchase, but which shared similar specifications. All three phones had the same wide-angle camera lens on the back, they all included the same A12 Bionic chip, they all had a notch along the top of the screen, and they all supported wireless charging.

However, the iPhone XR had an LCD screen that was bigger than the OLED display on the iPhone XS, but smaller than the display on the iPhone XS Max. Its frame was made from aluminium, rather than stainless steel, and it only had one camera on the back, instead of two. There were more differences, but for the average consumer, the iPhone XR was a much more attractive option than it's more expensive siblings. With its six color choices, it offered more personalization. Its 6.1-inch display was the perfect choice for those who couldn't decide between the smaller iPhone XS and its larger brother; and with its lower cost, the iPhone XR was more affordable for millions of people.

Chapter 1

Tech Specs

Internals:
Screen: 6.1" 1792x828 LCD
Processor: A12 Bionic
RAM: 3GB
Cameras: 12MP rear, 7MP front
Battery: 2942mAh
Storage: 64 / 128 / 256GB

Dimensions:
Height: 5.94"
Width: 2.98"
Thickness: 8.3mm
Weight: 194 grams

The plot thickens...

Until recently, every new iPhone was just a little bit thinner than its predecessor. To give an example, the iPhone 5 was 7.6mm thick, while the following iPhone 6 was just 6.9mm. For a time this was great for the consumer, because every time they upgraded to a new phone, it became a little bit smaller — and sometimes lighter too. Eventually, it became something of a problem, however, as the iPhone began to bend under considerable pressure, while phones slipped out of peoples hands. It seemed that people actually wanted thicker phones.

That began to happen with the iPhone X, and it continued with the XR. While the iPhone X, XS, and XS Max were all 7.7mm thick, the iPhone XR was 8.8mm thick. This gave Apple the opportunity to add more battery life, while massively improving the quality of the cameras.

Welcome

iPhone 11 Pro

All glass, better cameras, faster processor...

For those who want the most sophisticated technology available in a mobile phone, Apple has created something extraordinary: the iPhone 11 Pro.

It's called Pro for a reason because packed within its stainless steel and glass enclosure is the best triple-camera array available on any smartphone, the fastest mobile CPU, and the most advanced operating system available for a handheld device. Basically, if you rely on professional tools to get work done, then the iPhone 11 Pro is the device for you. It's also the choice of phone for anyone who simply wants the most advanced technology available.

Chapter 1

Design

The iPhone 11 Pro is the most advanced and detailed iPhone Apple has produced to date. Its outer-band is made from a surgical-grade stainless steel, while the back is a single piece of machined glass - even the area which surrounds the camera lenses. Run your finger along the back glass, and you'll notice that is has a beautiful matte finish, while the area around the cameras is polished and smooth. The new matte finish doesn't necessarily add any grip when you're holding the iPhone, but it makes it possible to tell which is the back and which is the front just by feel.

A brand new Midnight Green color has been introduced to the Pro range. In person it's a dark and smokey green, with just a hint of Boba Fett, but it changes depending on the lighting conditions. In sunlight, it's clearly green, but indoors it takes on neutral, almost dark grey appearance. Joining Midnight Green is the usual Space Grey, Silver, and Gold.

Super Retina XDR Display

There are two sizes of display to choose from when purchasing an iPhone 11 Pro:

iPhone 11 Pro
- 5.8" display
- 2436 x 1125 pixels
- 458 pixels-per-inch

iPhone 11 Pro Max
- 6.5" display
- 2688 x 1242 pixels
- 458 pixels-per-inch

Both have the highest pixel density of any product Apple makes, and both are packed with the most advanced technologies available, including:

Up to
800 nits
for better viewing in sunlight

Up to
1200 nits
for HDR Photos and 4K HDR movies

2,000,000:1
contrast ratio

458 pixels
per-nch

Wide color gamut
for incredible colors

Night Shift
for better viewing at night

True Tone
matches the white balance of the room

More efficient
by up to 15%

A small notch along the top of the display houses some of the most sophisticated technology ever developed for an iPhone. Called the TrueDepth Camera System, it contains the following sensors and emitters to enable facial recognition:

- Ambient light sensor
- Speaker
- Proximity Sensor
- Flood Illuminator

- Microphone
- 12MP camera
- Infrared Camera
- Dot Projector

Welcome

Cameras

This is the first camera system that Apple has assigned the word "Pro". It has a new wide camera, with a faster f/1.8 aperture and Focus Pixels covering 100% of the sensor. It has a new telephoto camera, with a larger 2.0 aperture which lets in 40% more light; and it has a brand new ultra-wide camera with a massive 120° field of view. All these cameras work in tandem with the A13 Bionic Chip, and a new generation signal processor, to enable an entirely new level of photography on a mobile device.

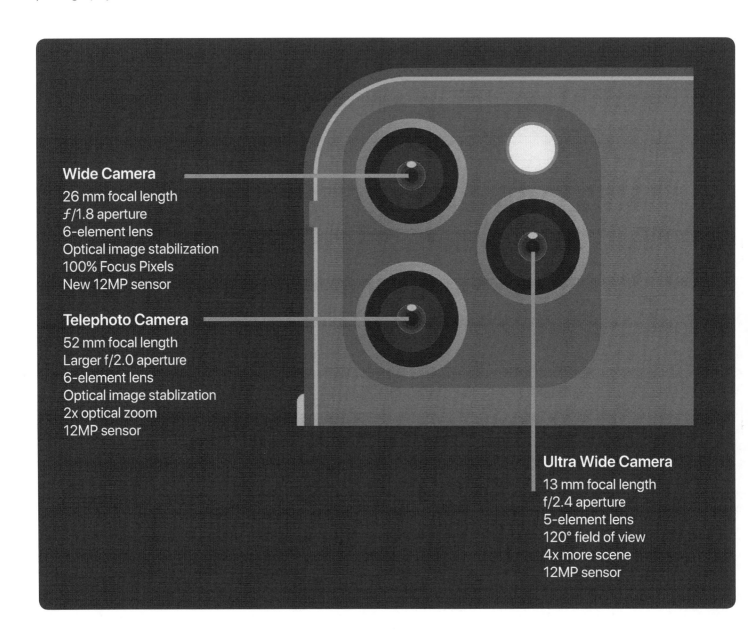

Wide Camera
26 mm focal length
ƒ/1.8 aperture
6-element lens
Optical image stabilization
100% Focus Pixels
New 12MP sensor

Telephoto Camera
52 mm focal length
Larger f/2.0 aperture
6-element lens
Optical image stablization
2x optical zoom
12MP sensor

Ultra Wide Camera
13 mm focal length
f/2.4 aperture
5-element lens
120° field of view
4x more scene
12MP sensor

The iPhone 11 Pro sensors also have a higher ISO range than previous iPhones (making them more sensitive in low light), plus a faster shutter speed; but the real improvements to image quality come from a 10-bit rendering pipeline, rather than an 8-bit pipeline. Apple calls this "semantic rendering"...

Semantic Rendering

Every time you take a photo on your iPhone, more than a trillion operations are calculated in a split second to ensure the image looks crisp and colorful. For the new iPhone, Apple has also added semantic rendering to the pipeline. It allows your iPhone to more intelligently detect subjects within an image, then light them with detail, ensuring your friends and family look even better than before. Here's how it works:

1. Your iPhone starts taking photos in the background as soon as you open the camera app, so by the time you press the shutter button, it has already captured four underexposed frames, plus the photo you want. It then grabs an additional overexposed frame.
2. Semantic rendering looks for things in the photos that it understands: such as faces, the sky, hair, water etc.
3. It uses detail from the underexposed and overexposed frames to selectively process those areas. So faces get illuminated, hair gets sharpened, and the sky is de-noised.
4. Semantic rendering is more selective when it comes to highlights and shadows, so highlights on faces aren't corrected as much, while shadows beneath trees are more corrected than before.
5. The entire image is saved to the Camera Roll, nearly instantly thanks to the A13 Bionic chip.

When it comes down to it, the iPhone 11 Pro takes sharper and more natural looking photos. It's difficult to compare the two in a 300 DPI print book, but if you were to take a selfie with an iPhone XS and an iPhone 11 Pro, you'll notice that the XS image looks a little hazier around the face, hair isn't quite so sharp, and overall there's just a little less detail.

Capture Outside the Frame

Open the Settings app and select Camera, and you'll notice two new options: "Photos Capture Outside the Frame" (off by default), and "Videos Capture Outside the Frame" (on by default).

When these options are enabled, the next time you shoot with either the 1x or 2x lenses, the Camera app will secretly use the next widest lens to capture additional footage outside of the frame. You won't see this footage until you edit the photo or video, then use the crop tool to rotate. Now, you can fix a wonky horizon without cropping the edges of the frame or zooming in.

Welcome

Night Mode xx

If you've owned an iPhone in the past (or nearly any type of mobile phone), then you've probably struggled to take a photo in low-light conditions. That's because the shutter needs to stay open for longer to capture the light, but if there's any movement, the image can be blurred and grainy. With the iPhone 11 Pro, the new wide camera system works in tandem with iOS and the A13 Bionic chips to capture detailed images in drastically lower light conditions.

Night Mode kicks in automatically when it's needed, like when you're taking a photo of the moon at night; so all you have to do is take a photo, and the iPhone will do all the work. It does this by taking multiple pictures, aligns them to correct for movement, discards any sections with blur, adjusts contrast so everything stays in balance, then de-noises the image to produce the final shot. Here are a few before and after shots to show you Dark Mode in action:

Chapter 1

Portrait Mode

Portrait Mode on the iPhone 11 Pro now works in both 1x and 2x view, so when using Portrait Mode you can snap between those two focal lengths (there's no way to pinch-to-zoom to something in-between, like 1.5x). The iPhone 11 Pro's telephoto lens also has an aperture of f/2.0, which means it's more sensitive in low light, so you can take better Portrait Mode photos in dim lighting (there's no Night Mode available in Portrait Mode, however).

With two camera lenses to work with, the iPhone 11 Pro can also work out the 3D space within an image, making it possible to take Portrait photos of nearly anything, like your pet dog, a flower, or a small object.

If you're wondering whether to use 1x or 2x for taking Portrait Mode photos, then here are a couple of tips:
- The 1x lens works better for small objects or pets.
- The 2x lens is better for taking flattering Portrait Mode photos of a person, especially if they're posing for the camera.

Front-Facing Camera

It's not just the back cameras that have received a major update for the iPhone 11 Pro, because the front-facing camera gets an all-new lens. It's called the TrueDepth Camera, and it's now 12MP, making your selfies and front-facing videos sharper and more rich than ever before.

However, there's a slight catch to the new 12MP lens. When you're taking a shot in portrait mode, the image is only 7MP in size. It's not until you rotate your iPhone 11 into landscape mode that the 12MP image kicks-in; so basically, if you want to capture more of the world around you when using the front-facing camera, hold your iPhone horizontally.

The front-facing camera can now record 4K video, with HDR lighting at 30 frames-per-second, or standard lighting at 60 frames-per-second. You can toggle between modes by using the Settings app. Apple has also added the ability to record slow-motion video using the front-facing camera, so you can capture a slow-motion selfie (or Slofie, as Apple calls them) and share it with friends.

Welcome

Battery Life

Ask any previous iPhone owner what they wished for most in their next iPhone, and the number one request would probably be better battery life. We've all encountered moments where our iPhone needs charging before the end of the day; some even go so far as to carry a battery pack with them for emergency top-ups. Apple has been listening to these complaints, and they've managed to squeeze an extra four hours of battery life out of the iPhone 11 Pro (when compared to the iPhone XS), and a really impressive five hours from the iPhone 11 Pro Max (when compared to the XS Max). It has managed to do this with a couple of changes that affect both the hardware and software.

The first change was to make both iPhones a little thicker and a little heavier. The iPhone 11 Pro is 0.01 inch (0.4mm) thicker and 0.3 ounces (11 grams) heavier than the iPhone XS. You probably won't notice if you're comparing them side-by-side, but if you're upgrading from an older iPhone (such as the iPhone 7) then the 11 Pro is 1.7 ounces (50 grams) heavier. You'll definitely notice that extra weight.

Apple also removed support for 3D Touch, instead replacing it with Haptic Touch (basically, a long press). 3D Touch was originally introduced with the iPhone 6s. Every new iPhone afterwards included it, with the exception of the iPhone SE - until the iPhone XR was released in 2018. It was a novel feature that enabled users to press firmly on the display to access additional menus, settings and features. Take the Home Screen for example. By pressing firmly on an app icon it was possible to access a secondary menu offering shortcuts to various features within an app, so press firmly on the Camera app, and you could jump straight into video recording mode or take a selfie. 3D Touch never really took off for various reasons. First, it was undiscoverable - there was no way to know what button or app supported 3D Touch. Second, the feature replicated a long touch in a few areas, making it confusing as to when to firm press and when to long press. By removing 3D Touch, Apple has managed to free an entire layer of sensors beneath the display - in turn freeing up space for a thicker battery.

Water Resistence

The iPhone 11 Pro is Apple's most water resistant iPhone yet.

IP68 rating
water resistant to a depth of 4 meters for up to 30 minutes.

Spill resistant
for common liquids like coffee, tea, soda, and even beer

Dust resistant
thanks to precision-fitted seals around the buttons.

A13 Bionic

Apple is fairly unique in the mobile phone industry in that it owns the entire vertical stack of technology used within the iPhone. If you're unfamiliar with the term "vertical stack" it means Apple owns the software which powers the iPhone, the CPU design, and many of the smaller components which all come together to form an iPhone. This enables the company to optimize the entire flow of both hardware and software to make the fastest mobile devices in the industry. For the iPhone 11 Pro, Apple has introduced the A13 Bionic Chip - Apple's next-generation chipset, and the fastest CPU ever in a smartphone. When it comes to machine learning, the A13 Bionic is capable of performing more than 1 trillion operations per second, which means the iPhone 11 Pro can recognize objects quicker, scan photos for faces faster, and perform other machine learning tasks required by the latest apps. At Apple's September Event 2019, the company produced these benchmark results to compare the iPhone with its nearest competitors:

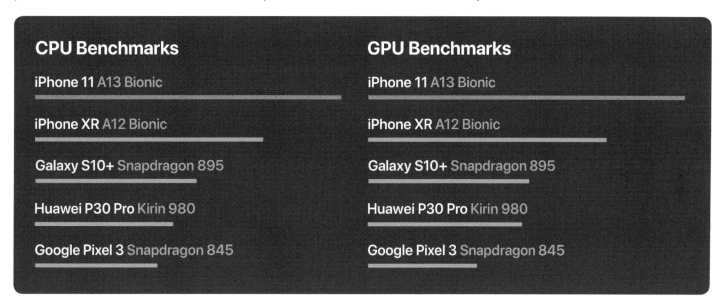

The A13 Bionic is also Apples most power-efficient chip to date. To do this, the chip is packed with 8.5 billion transistors, each one being an advanced, second-generation 7-nanometer design. Each transistor is carefully tailored for high-performance while requiring low power, which means you can expect to receive up to 5 more hours of battery life when compared to the iPhone XS Max.

Audio

The iPhone 11 Pro features a new audio technology called Spacial Audio. It provides an immersive theatre-like experience by creating a sound field around you, using an Apple-designed virtualizer. Basically, it's now possible to create the impression of audio in front, to the side, and behind you. Spacial Audio supports 5.1 and 7.1 surround (Netflix will play in Dolby Digital 5.1), alongside Dolby Atmos in movies purchased from the iTunes store. Both speakers are now louder than ever too.

Welcome

iPhone 11

Almost the same as the 11 Pro, but more affordable…

Announced alongside the iPhone 11 Pro, the iPhone 11 is the ideal phone for those who want the most sophisticated technology available in a mobile phone, but without a sky-high price.

It takes everything that's great about the 11 Pro then cuts a few corners to save literately hundreds of $£€; so the iPhone 11 features 2 camera lenses, rather than 3, an LCD display, rather than an OLED, and a maximum storage option of 256GB, rather than 512GB.

On this spread we'll take a look at the two big differences between the 11 and the 11 Pro: the display and the camera. For a wider look at how the two sets of phones compare, flick over to the next page.

Chapter 1

Liquid Retina Display

Rather than including an OLED display like the iPhone 11 Pro, the 11 features an LCD with the following specs:

6.1" display
at a resolution of 1792 x 828

P3
wide color display

1400:1
contrast ratio

326 pixels
per-nch

Wide color gamut
for incredible colors

Night Shift
for better viewing at night

True Tone
matches the white balance of the room

625 nits
for better viewing in sunlight

One less camera lens

The iPhone 11 has a double lens array on the back, so it's missing the telescopic 2x lens found on the 11 Pro:

Wide Camera
26 mm focal length
ƒ/1.8 aperture
6-element lens
Optical image stabilization
100% Focus Pixels
New 12MP sensor

Ultra Wide Camera
13 mm focal length
f/2.4 aperture
5-element lens
120° field of view
4x more scene
12MP sensor

Welcome

Pro, or no go Pro?

Is the $300 price difference justified between the iPhone 11 and the 11 Pro?

Every year it gets a little bit harder to decide whether to go for the "super tier" iPhone or the "regular" iPhone. 2019 might be the most challenging year yet because, on a technical level, the only differences between the iPhone 11 and the iPhone 11 Pro seem to be:

* Three cameras around the back, rather than two.
* An OLED display, rather than an LCD.
* Slightly faster LTE.
* Different choice of colors.
* More storage.

Some might gawk at those differences and say they don't justify the extra cost. Maybe they're right. We all have different priorities and tastes. The iPhone 11 Pro is aimed at two types of people: those who cherish quality over price, and those who genuinely need more storage and a telephoto lens for professional work.

There's an argument for both sides. After-all, there is a genuine professional argument to be made for the iPhone 11 Pro's camera system. The additional telescopic lens makes it possible to capture people, objects and landscapes further away, with a true 2X zoom. It also has an f/2.0 aperture instead of the f/2.4 found on the iPhone XS Max. If you're hoping to replace your DSLR with your iPhone, or shoot professional-looking video on the go, then the iPhone 11 Pro is a genuine replacement for most people.

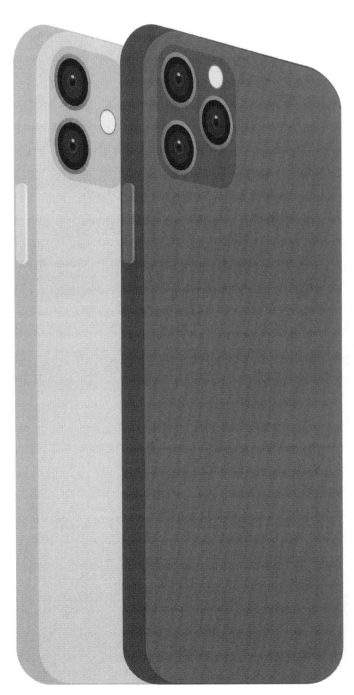

When it comes to battery life, the iPhone 11 Pro Max is the clear winner. It manages to last up to 5 hours longer than last years iPhone XS Max, while the iPhone 11 Pro gets an additional 4 hours of battery life. The iPhone 11 squeezes an additional 1 hour of battery life when compared to last years iPhone XR. Impressive when you consider the XR had the longest battery life of any iPhone in 2018.

When it comes to color, well that's definitely a personal choice. Some will prefer the pastel-like colors of the iPhone 11, while others will crave the smokey palette of the 11 Pro. In-person, the Midnight Green has a grungy feel that's part military and part Boba Fest; while the iPhone 11's purple, yellow, and green finishes are more bright and cheerful. The back glass panels are impressive across the board, all being milled down from a single piece of glass. On the iPhone 11 Pro, the back has a matte finish with the camera area being polished; while on the iPhone 11, it's the reverse, so the back is polished while the camera area is matte.

Welcome

Wondering which iPhone to get?

Some helpful tips for deciding whether to go XR, 11, Pro, or Max…

The iPhone is the most popular mobile in the world, but it comes in a variety of sizes, colors, and specifications. Choosing the right one for you isn't just determined by cost, but also what you want to get out of the phone. Here are some tips and pointers to help you decide…

"All I need is the basics"

If you just want to make calls, check emails, browse the web, and look at Facebook, then the iPhone XR, in it's smallest storage capacity (64GB), is the best iPhone for you. Now all you need to do is pick a color. You can choose from white, black, blue, yellow, coral, and (PRODUCT) RED™.

"I want the best for photography"

The iPhone XR doesn't include a telescopic lens for taking photos of things in the distance, so it's automatically ruled out here. It's also less accurate when taking Portrait Mode photos. What you want is either an iPhone 11 or an 11 Pro. Both include an Ultra Wide lens. Go 11 Pro and you also get a 2X telescopic lens too, which is great for capturing things in the distance.

"I'm pretty creative and/or productive"

If you're going to use your iPhone for manipulating videos, editing photos, writing documents, or anything else which involves making things, then the iPhone 11 Pro Max is the model of choice. It has the biggest screen, so creating anything is easier to do, and it also supports landscape mode in a variety of apps, making the keyboard larger too.

Chapter 1

"I want the best iPhone without spending a fortune"

If you're looking for the best iPhone, but don't want to spend upwards of a thousand $/£/€, then go for the iPhone 11. The only major differences between the 11 and the Pro are 2 cameras instead of 3, an OLED display rather then LCD, and slightly slower LTE.

"I want the biggest and most expensive iPhone"

If you're going to use your iPhone for watching movies, enjoying photos, or doing anything productive, and you also want the "best of the best", then go for the iPhone 11 Pro Max. It's the biggest, the shiniest, and the most expensive of all the iPhones.

Welcome

Cases and screen protectors

Learn about the many ways you can protect your iPhone...

You've probably seen a lot of iPhones in cases. Not only do they protect an iPhone from drops and bangs, but they can also add a personal touch to a device which can look a little "industrial". Whether you need a case is down to personal use. If you have ever dropped your iPhone, then a case is probably a good idea. If you're the kind of human who takes extra of your mobile, who always carefully places it onto soft surfaces and keeps it away from keys and other sharp objects, then a case or screen protector is probably unnecessary.

Official Apple Cases

iPhone Silicon Case   iPhone Leather Case   iPhone Leather Folio

If you've wandered into an Apple Store, then you might have noticed the row upon row of iPhone cases along one side of the wall. They come in two finishes: leather or silicone.

The official Apple leather cases are really quite good. They're sturdy, feel pleasant to touch, and age well. On the downside, they're rather expensive. Opt for a leather Apple case if you want to go the "premium" route, and plan to use your case for a long time.

The silicone cases feel amazing when they're new. Think of butter, but not as wet and sticky, and you'll get the idea. Over time the official silicone cases start to go shiny and slippery. It's an ugly look, so go with one of these if you're planning to swap your case on a regular basis.

Unofficial cases

There are literately thousands of third-party cases to choose from. Some are transparent, some use rigid plastic, other mimic the official Apple cases - and do a really good job at it. If you can't decide what case to buy or need some helpful tips, then this is what you should look for:

Think about what level of protection you need. If you have children or an active lifestyle, then something thick and sturdy is what you need. If you want minimal protection, then look for a "skin" case. If it's fashion you're after, then any type of case should work. Just look for the right color, texture, pattern, or bling.

Read user reviews. Some cases might fall apart after a few weeks, or they might scratch an iPhone as the case is put on. Some might even block the camera if they're poorly designed or manufactured.

Go cheap if you can't decide on a color. Some third-party cases are the price of a latte, so you can go wild and buy them in a range of colors, then swap the cases around depending on your mood or outfit.

Screen Protectors

For most people, screen protectors are a waste of time. That's because iPhones have always used Gorilla Glass for the front of the device. Gorilla Glass is incredibly strong. It's used for the windshields of helicopters, and it's able to deflect dings and scratches from even the toughest of materials. Every year the materialists at Gorilla Glass improve the formula used to manufacture the glass too, so it gets stronger and stronger with each new iPhone. Unless you use your phone in a hazardous environment, keep your iPhone alongside keys, or have small children who enjoy watching videos on your iPhone, then a screen protector is only going to hinder the visual quality of the display, rather than protect it.

That being said, if you'd like to use a screen protector, make sure it's the exact size and type for your iPhone. That's because there are subtle differences between the standard iPhone, the Max, and the R models. Also look for a screen protector which includes an applicator of sorts. They usually look like small blank credit cards. This will help you eliminate any bubbles from getting stuck under the screen protector as you apply it to the screen.

The Basics

The iPhone raises the bar for smartphone technology, but it's just as intuitive and delightful to use as all previous iPhones. This chapter will cover the very basics of using iPhone. You'll discover its gestures, how to access Control Center, and much more.

Contents:

Setup and activate your iPhone	42
Face ID	44
The Lock Screen	46
The Home Screen	47
Gestures and Buttons	48
Connect to a Wi-Fi network	50
iCloud	51
How to use Control Center	52
Display Settings	54
Toggle Dark Mode	56
How to use Spotlight	58
How to manage Notifications	60
Talk to Siri	62
Accounts, emails, and passwords	64
Type like a Pro	66
How to cut, copy and paste	68
How to use the Share sheet	70
Use AirDrop to share files	71
Data Roaming & Personal Hotspots	72
Use Handoff to work between devices	74
Emergency SOS	75
Use Apple Pay to buy things	76
Use AirPlay to stream content to a TV	78

The Basics

Setup and activate your iPhone

Discover how to activate your brand new iPhone...

So you've bought a shiny new iPhone, and you've unwrapped it from the box. What next?

The first thing you need to do is to insert a SIM card. This will let your iPhone connect to the web and activate itself.

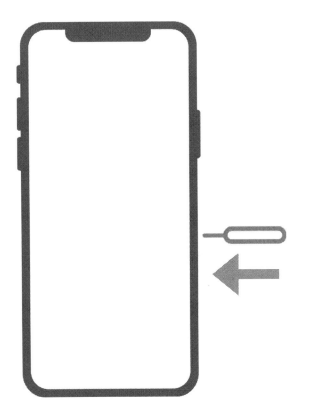

How to insert a SIM card

1. Look in the iPhone box for the SIM tray tool. It's thin, silver, and looks like a paperclip.

2. Insert the pointy end of the SIM tray tool into the small hole on the right-side of your iPhone.

3. Press hard, and the sim tray will pop out slightly.

3. Use your fingernail to pull the sim tray out, then carefully place your SIM card into it. You might have to flip it around to make sure it fits property.

4. Slide the SIM tray back into your iPhone and you're good to go.

How to activate your iPhone

1. Start by turning on your iPhone for the first time. To do this, just press the **power** button on the upper-right side. After a moment or two the Apple logo will appear.

2. When the Hello screen appears, **swipe up** from the bottom of the screen to continue.

3. Tap the language you want to use for your iPhone, then tap the country or region.

Chapter 2

Use the Quick Start tool to copy across your old iPhone

If you're going from an old iPhone to a new one, then you can use the Quick Start tool to automatically copy across all of your messages, photos, apps, settings, and personal data to the new iPhone. It works quickly and it's easy to do...

Before you begin...

If you have an Apple Watch, make sure to unpair it from your old iPhone before you set up the new one. To do this open the **Apple Watch** app, tap **My Watch**, select your watch, tap the **info** button then tap **Unpair Apple Watch**. You can re-pair it to the new device during the setup process.

Then...

1. Place your new iPhone next to your old one. The Quick Start screen will automatically offer the option of using your Apple ID to set up the new device. Make sure it's the right Apple ID, then tap **Continue**.

2. Wait for an animation to appear on your new iPhone, then use the camera viewfinder on the old iPhone and center the animation in the middle of the screen. When you see a button that says **Finish on New [Device]**, tap the button and follow the on-screen options to transfer your apps, data, and settings to the new device.

3. If you have an Apple Watch, you'll be asked if you would like to transfer your Apple Watch data and settings too.

Use the Quick Start tool to copy your data from iCloud

If you don't have your old iPhone to hand, then you can sync all of your messages, apps, accounts, and other personal data from iCloud. To do this:

1. After activating your iPhone, tap **Restore from iCloud Backup**.

2. Sign into iCloud using your Apple ID and password.

3. Choose the most recent backup. You can check by looking at the date and size of each backup.

4. If you've purchased apps and iTunes content using multiple Apple IDs then you'll be asked for the passwords to each one.

5. Wait for the process to finish. This may take some time, so it's a good idea to keep your device connected to Wi-Fi and a power source.

6. After the process has completed your device will turn on and activate, but it will still need to download content such as apps and photos, so be patient as it restores all of your data.

The Basics

Face ID

Learn how to setup Face ID so you can unlock your iPhone using your face…

One of the most sci-fi features of the iPhone is its ability to instantly scan your face with a dot projector, then automatically unlock it or let you buy things. It's a feature called Face ID, and it's way more advanced than you might think.

It works by using a TrueDepth Camera System to recognize you. Basically, an infrared camera can see your face, even in the dark, while a dot projector maps your face with more than 30,000 dots. All of this data is used to create a mathematical model of your face. This mathematical model is used to prevent people from using photos of you to unlock your iPhone. Face ID also looks for telltale signs of life (like moving or blinking eyes), to know that a model of your face wasn't used. Once it has confirmed all of this (which usually takes less than a second) then Face ID tells your iPhone that it's definitely you; and that things are good to go.

Here's a neat little fact: when using Face ID, there's a 1 in a million chance that someone else can unlock your device by looking at it.

Chapter 2

How to set up Face ID

1

Your iPhone will ask you to setup Face ID when you activate it for the very first time. If you skipped that step, just open the **Settings** app, select **Face ID & Passcode** then tap **Enrol Face.**

2

Follow the on-screen instructions to add your face. You'll be asked to gently move your head in a circular motion. That's because Face ID performs best when all angles of your face are captured.

3

Once the process is complete, tap **Done** to enrol your face.

How to quickly disable Face ID

Press the **power** button five times and your iPhone will enter Emergency SOS mode. This disables Face ID, meaning you can only unlock your iPhone using your six-digit passcode.

Set up an alternative look

If you sometimes change your look in a drastic way (for example via makeup, with a wig, or with extensive accessories), then you can teach Face ID to recognize you with these changes. To do this, get ready with your alternative look, then go to **Settings > Face ID & Passcode**, then tap **Set Up an Alternate Appearance**.

45

The Basics

The Lock Screen

Use gestures to unlock your iPhone, access Notification Center, and more...

Lift up your iPhone and (so long as it's turned on) the Lock Screen will quickly fade into view. If you've received any notifications, such as a text message or a news story, then you'll see them in the middle of the screen. Otherwise, you'll just see the background wallpaper, time, and date.

If your iPhone is on a desk and you don't want to pick it up, then you can also tap on the screen to display the Lock Screen.

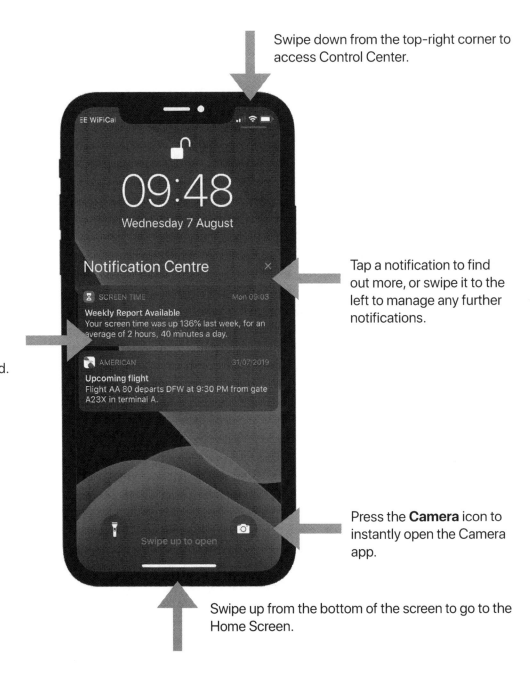

Swipe down from the top-right corner to access Control Center.

Tap a notification to find out more, or swipe it to the left to manage any further notifications.

Swipe from the left to access Spotlight, where all your widgets, shortcuts and Spotlight search can be found.

Press the **Camera** icon to instantly open the Camera app.

Swipe up from the bottom of the screen to go to the Home Screen.

Chapter 2

The Home Screen

Discover how to interact with apps and folders...

Delete an app

If you've downloaded an app but want to remove it, simply tap and hold on the app icon, then tap the **cross** button that appears when the app starts to wiggle.

Move apps

To rearrange an app on the home screen of your device, **tap and hold** on its icon, then slide the app to wherever you wish to place it. Tap **Done** in the top corner to confirm.

Create a folder of apps

Simply **tap and hold** on an app, then drag it on top of another app. This will create a folder of apps. You can rename a folder by tapping and holding on its name.

Wondering what those icons at the top of the screen mean?

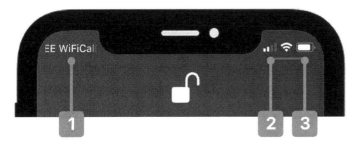
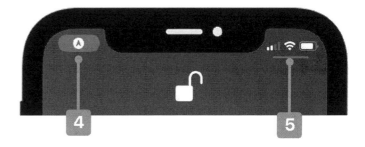

1. The name of your service provider will appear here. In this example, it's EE.

2. These five vertical lines represents the signal strength of your carrier, so the more filled-in circles you see, the stronger the signal.

3. This icon displays how much battery life remains. You can toggle a percentage count on and off by opening the **Settings** app and going to **Battery** > **Battery Percentage.**

4. This icon appears when an app is tracking your location. For example, you might be using the Maps app, or perhaps a fitness app that monitors your distance and speed.

5. This center icon on the right-side of the screen will either display your network connection type, or Wi-Fi strength.

The Basics

Gestures and Buttons

Learn about key gestures used for controlling your iPhone...

The vast, high-definition screen that spreads out across your iPhone is a technological marvel. You might not know it, but it actually supports up to 10 individual fingertips, and works by detecting the static charge on your skin — not heat or pressure as many often believe. By tapping and gesturing on the screen you can take full advantage of everything iOS has to offer, such as zooming into content, rotating images and more. Additionally, the hardware buttons on your iPhone enable you to access Apple Pay, activate Siri or shut the entire thing off. Many of these functions are entirely intuitive, but for those who have never interacted with an iPhone before, let's go over them...

Return to the Home screen

Whenever you're in an app, swipe up from the very bottom of the screen to return to the Home screen.

Access the multitasking screen

Swipe up from the bottom of the screen then stop halfway to see all the apps you've recently opened. You can scroll through the app thumbnails, then tap on one to re-open it.

Force quit an app

While you're viewing the multitasking screen, push an app thumbnail upwards and off the screen to force quit it. You only need to do this if an app has crashed and stopped working.

Chapter 2

Access Siri

To talk to Siri - your personal voice-activated assistant - just press and hold the **Power** button on the side of your iPhone.

Power off your device

If you'd like to fully turn off your iPhone, then hold down both the **power** button and **volume up** buttons.

Access Apple Pay

To quickly pull up your debit and credit cards, double-press the **Power** button on the side of your iPhone.

Jump between apps

Want to quickly jump between apps? Swipe along the very bottom of the screen, left-to-right, and you'll jump between apps.

Access Search

From the Home screen, pull the screen down using your finger to access the Search screen appear. From here you can search for apps, emails, contacts and more. You'll also see app and web search suggestions based on your history and recent activity.

Swipe to go back

Want to go back a panel or page? Just swipe from the left-side of the screen inwards and you'll go back to the previous area. This works great for going back a page in Safari, or for going back to your Mailboxes in the Mail app.

49

The Basics

Connect to a Wi-Fi network

Easily connect to home, office, or public Wi-Fi networks...

Connecting to a Wi-Fi network is one of those fundamental tasks that we all must do from time to time. Perhaps you're visiting a friend and would like to hook up to their internet connection, or you might be sat in a coffee shop that offers free Wi-Fi. Here's how to do it:

1. Open the **Settings** app then tap the **Wi-Fi** button.

2. If Wi-Fi isn't already turned on then tap the toggle button near the top of the screen.

3. Select a wireless network, and enter its password if necessary.

4. Tap the blue **Join** button on the keyboard. If you've entered the password successfully your device will automatically join the network.

Public networks

If the network doesn't require a password, then you can just tap on the Wi-Fi network name and immediately connect. Note, however, that sometimes networks require you to enter personal details via the Safari app before you can freely browse the web. You'll probably come across this situation in coffee shops and airports. Hotels might also request you to enter your hotel room number and a password, the latter of which is typically available from the reception.

Share a Wi-Fi password

Looking for the Wi-Fi password is always a pain. It's usually hidden on the back of a router, printed on an obscure piece of card or written in small print on a receipt. Over time this becomes less of a problem, as Wi-Fi passwords are stored in your iCloud account, so once you connect to a network all of your devices will automatically join when they come within reach; but nevertheless, those new networks will still appear every now and then.

With the Share Wi-Fi feature, joining wireless networks becomes slightly easier, because you can automatically copy Wi-Fi passwords from one iOS device to another. Here's how it works:

1. Enter the range of a new WiFi network.

2. Place your iPhone near an unlocked iOS device that's already connected to the Wi-Fi network.

3. Your iPhone will automatically ask the other device for the Wi-Fi password.

4. If the owner of the other device agrees to the request, then you'll receive the password automatically and instantly connect.

Chapter 2

iCloud

Learn what iCloud is all about...

iCloud enables you to sync all of your images, videos, music, apps, contacts, calendars and much more across your iPhone and Mac or PC. This means you can snap a photo on your iPhone then see it automatically appear on your Mac, PC, or television. It means you can purchase a song, movie or TV show in iTunes, and see it appear on all of your Apple devices. It means you can start writing a document on your Mac, edit it on your iPhone, and see the changes appear across both devices. You can also backup your iPhone wirelessly, see where your friends are on a map, sync bookmarks and much more.

Photos

Any photos taken on your iPhone are wirelessly uploaded to iCloud, then automatically downloaded onto your other iOS devices, Mac and/or PC. So you can take a photo during the day on your iPhone, then get home and view it larger on your Mac, all without having to sync or use wires.

iCloud Drive

iCloud Drive automatically saves all your documents created in Pages, Keynote, Numbers and Notes, then wirelessly beams them to your other devices. So if you're writing a letter or creating a presentation on your Mac, you'll be able to continue editing it on your iPad or iPhone without having to worry about saving it or transferring the file. Edits are automatically updated across all of your devices too. It works like magic. To access all the files in your iCloud Drive, simply open the **Files** app then select **iCloud Drive**.

Find My iPhone

If you can't find your iPhone, Find My iPhone will enable you to track it through iCloud. By signing into your iCloud account, either from www.icloud.com or another iPhone, you can see your devices on a map, set a passcode lock, remotely wipe them or send a message to the screen. You can also enable Lost Mode, whereby the device is automatically locked, a message with a contact appears on the screen and the device automatically tracks where it's been and reports it back to Find My iPhone.

Safari

iCloud automatically saves your bookmarks, Reading Lists and open tabs. So if you're reading a lengthy web article on your Mac but need to dash, you can continue reading it at a later time on your iPhone. To do this open **Safari** on your iPhone, tap on the **Tabs** button, then scroll up to see every tab open on all of your Apple devices.

Backup

iCloud automatically backs up your iPhone when it's plugged into a power source and connected to the web over Wi-Fi. iCloud backs up the following things: music, movies, TV shows, apps, books, photos and videos in the Camera Roll, device settings, app data, ringtones, app organization and messages. And if you buy a new iPhone, you can restore all of the above by using an existing iCloud backup.

The Basics

How to use Control Center

Discover how to quickly toggle controls…

Tucked above the screen are a helpful set of shortcut buttons for toggling common switches and settings. They include a slider for controlling the screen brightness, a button for enabling Wi-Fi, shortcuts to toggle Airplane Mode, Night Shift mode and more. To access these shortcuts at any time swipe down from the top-right corner of the screen. In an instant, you'll see Control Center appear as an overlay above the screen.

All of the toggles and buttons in Control Center support Haptic Touch to show you further settings or more extensive controls. To use Haptic Touch on a button just tap and hold and it will expand beneath your finger.

To close Control Center swipe back up or tap in the empty space below Control Center.

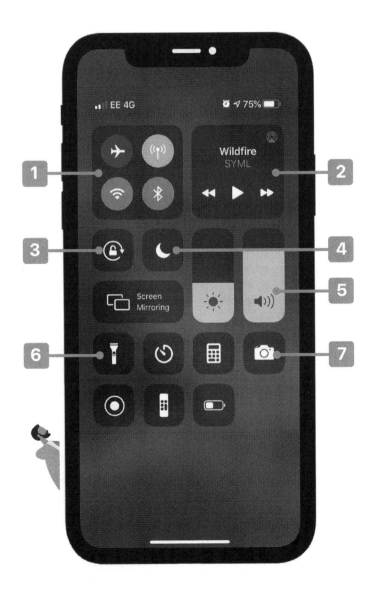

1 Network and connection settings

The rounded box in the top-left corner of the screen is where you can access all the wireless and network settings for your iPhone. By default, you'll see four controls for activating or disabling Airplane mode, your cellular connection, Wi-Fi and Bluetooth. By tapping and holding on this box, you can also access controls for AirDrop and Personal Hotspot.

2 Music controls

The box in the upper-right portion of the screen lets you control music playback and settings. By default you'll see the track name, play, and fast-forward/skip. If you have headphones connected, then in the top-right corner of the box will be a small icon (it looks like two curved lines) for choosing the playback device. Tap and hold on the music controls box to expand it to show album artwork, a volume slider, and a timeline scrubber.

3 Orientation Lock

If you don't want the screen to rotate into landscape/portrait mode when you rotate the device, tap the **Orientation Lock** button.

4 Do Not Disturb

Tap the **moon** icon to turn on Do Not Disturb. While it's on you won't be bothered by phone calls, texts or any notifications, your device won't emit any noise and the screen won't turn on.
Tap and hold on this button and you'll be able to access various shortcuts to enable Do Not Disturb for a period of time, or until you leave a location.

5 Brightness and volume sliders

To the middle-right of Control Center are sliders for adjusting the device brightness and volume. Drag these sliders to change the screen brightness or volume, or tap and hold to access larger controls that are easier to use.

6 Flashlight

Tap the **Torch** icon to instantly turn on the flash at the back of your iPhone. You can also tap and hold to choose between bright, medium and low settings.

7 App shortcuts

Tap the **Timer**, **Calculator** or **Camera** button to instantly open these apps. You can also tap and hold to activate features such as the flashlight brightness, timer length and video recording.

Customize Control Center

If you want to add additional buttons to Control Center, or remove those that you don't use very often, simply open the **Settings** app and tap **Control Center.** On the following panel you'll find shortcuts to add and remove options. You can also rearrange the options by using the drag buttons to customize Control Center to your exact needs.

The Basics

Display Settings

Learn how to adjust the display to meet your needs...

The display of your iPhone is its most crucial component, because it's the one you spend the most time prodding, poking, and stroking. Without a screen, the iPhone wouldn't be much better than one of those old rotary-dial phones. Tucked away in both Control Center and the Settings app are some helpful controls which let you adjust the screen to suit your needs better. You can play around with the brightness, enable True Tone, and capture what's on the screen to share with others...

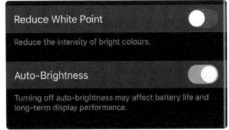

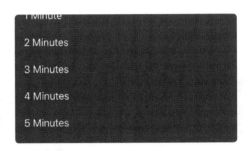

Adjust the brightness

If you'd like to adjust the brightness of the display, just swipe down from the top-right corner of the screen to access Control Center, then slide the brightness slider up or down. You can also tap and hold on the slider to enable a larger version that's easier to control.

Disable Auto-Brightness

By default your iPhone will automatically adjust the brightness of the display to match the conditions of your environment; so if you're in a dark room, the screen will dim, while under direct sunlight it will set to maximum brightness.
To turn this off or on, go to **Settings > Accessibility > Display & Text Size** and turn **Auto-Brightness** off.

Adjust the Auto-Timer

If you'd like to adjust how long it takes until your iPhone locks, go to **Settings > Display & Brightness > Auto-Lock**, where you'll find several settings that range from 1 minute to never.

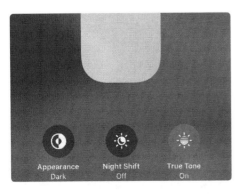

Disable True Tone

True Tone is a brilliant feature that adjusts the screen ambience to match the environment around you. So if you're sitting in a room with yellowish light, the screen will subtly change to suit the environment.

If you prefer the screen to always look pure white, open the **Settings** app and go to **Display & Brightness,** then toggle **True Tone** off. You can also disable True Tone from Control Center. Just tap and hold on the brightness slider, then tap the **True Tone** button.

Chapter 2

Take a screenshot

If you want to share something interesting on your screen then taking a screenshot of it is a great way to do this. Here's how it works:

1 Press the **Power** button and **Volume Up** buttons at the same time to capture the screen.

2 You'll see a thumbnail of the screenshot minimize and snap to the bottom left corner.

3 Leave the thumbnail alone for a few seconds and it will disappear and save the screenshot to the Photos app. You can also swipe the thumbnail to the left to quickly save it.

4 Tap on the thumbnail and you can annotate it or delete it.

5 Tap and hold on the thumbnail and you can easily share it with friends and contacts, print it or even create a watch face.

Create a video recording of the screen

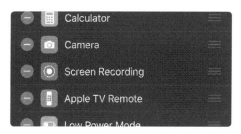

Start by adding the Screen Recording widget to Control Center. To do this go to **Settings > Control Center > Customize Controls** then add **Screen Recording**.

Close the Settings app and swipe down from the top-right corner to enable Control Center.

Tap the **Screen Recording** button (it looks like the outline of a circle with a dot in the middle) and after three seconds the recording will begin.

Tap the red bar at the top of the screen to stop the recording.

To capture audio, tap and hold on the **Screen Recording** button within Control Center, then tap **Microphone Audio**.

55

The Basics

Toggle Dark Mode

Give your apps an evocative new look...

With Dark Mode you can turn to the dark side by giving all the default apps an evocative new look. Basically, whites become black, folder backgrounds and the Dock take on a smokey look, and even the default wallpapers supplied by Apple take on a darker look.

Enable Dark Mode

There are two ways you can turn on (or off) Dark Mode:

1 Access Control Center, tap and hold on the brightness slider, then tap the **Appearance** button in the bottom-left corner.

2 Open the **Settings** app, select **Display & Brightness**, then tap the **Dark** option at the top of the screen.

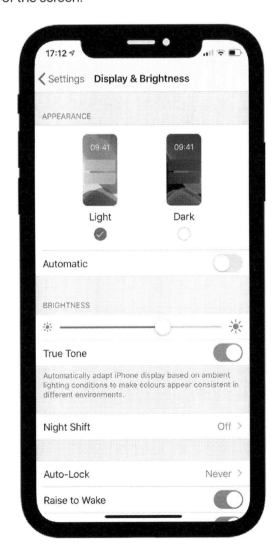

Chapter 2

Dark Mode comparisons...

Lock screen

Safari

Notes

Maps

The Basics

How to use Spotlight

Search your phone, or quickly access app widgets...

You might not realize, but your iPhone knows a lot about your daily schedule and lifestyle. It's continually monitoring your calendar schedule, physical activity, messages, commute, and more. Don't worry, this data isn't used for nefarious reasons; instead, it's used by the operating system to help you get home on time, achieve your fitness goals, meet all your appointments and more; all via the Spotlight screen.

How to access Spotlight

There are three ways to access the Spotlight screen:

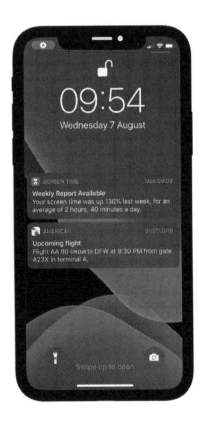  

Just raise your iPhone or press the **power** button and any new spotlight information will appear on the Lock Screen. These might include new messages, map directions or your next calendar appointment.

From the Home screen, swipe to the right and the Spotlight widget panel will appear.

From the Home screen, swipe down from the middle of the screen and the Spotlight search panel will appear.

Chapter 2

Spotlight Widgets

From the Home screen, swipe to the right to access a panel of Spotlight widgets. Each widget is a small panel of helpful information. You might see the latest news stories, app suggestions, steps walked during the day, or unread emails.

Some widgets can be expanded to show more detail. You'll know because there will be a **small arrow** in the top-right corner of the widget. Tap this button and the widget will expand to reveal more information.

Edit Spotlight Widgets

By customizing the Spotlight widget panel, you can add your favorite widgets, or clear away any which you don't find helpful. To do this, swipe down to the bottom of the Spotlight panel, then tap the **Edit** button. On the following screen you can add, delete, and reorder widgets to suit your needs.

Unnecessary Tip!

Don't microwave your iPhone.

It doesn't taste as nice as you'd think. Also, it'll blow up your microwave.

The Basics

How to manage Notifications

Discover how to manage notifications…

However you use your iPhone, you're going to receive notifications on a regular basis. Notifications usually appear when you have a new message, or if an app wants to get your attention. If your iPhone is locked, then the notification will appear as a bubble on the Lock Screen. If you're using your device when the notification arrives, then it will appear as a floating panel at the top of the screen. If an app wants to get your attention, then you might see a red dot above its icon on the Home screen.

If there's one annoying aspect about receiving notifications on an iPhone, it's that you can't simply ignore them. Try to do that, and they'll only end up in the Notification Center, forever awaiting an action from yourself. Try and ignore that little red dot above an app icon, and it'll never go away. Thankfully, you can customize, hide, and even disable notifications from individual apps…

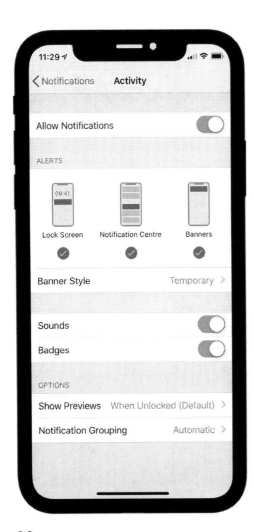

Change how notifications appear

To change an alert style for a notification, go to **Settings > Notifications**, then select an app. Here are some of the alert styles you can choose from:

- **Allow Notifications:** Toggle on to receive notifications from the app you selected.

- **Banners:** Choose how you want notifications to appear when your iPhone is unlocked. Tap **Temporary** to display alerts for a short period of time, or tap **Persistent** to have alerts stay on the screen until you act on it.

- **Sounds:** Toggle sound alerts for when you receive a notification.

- **Show on Lock Screen:** Turn on to see notifications on your Lock screen.

- **Show in History:** See previous notifications from the app you selected.

- **Show Previews:** Choose what you want to see when you get a notification, like a text message.

Chapter 2

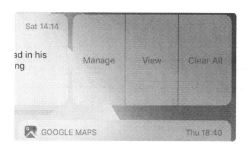

Clear all your notifications at once

If you have a stack of notifications waiting for you in Notification Center, then you can clear them all at once by swiping the stack to the left then choosing **Clear All.**

Interact with notifications

If a notification appears while you're using your iPhone, pull it down from the top of the screen using your finger to interact with it. For example, if you get a message, pull the notification down and you'll be able to send a reply without going into the Messages app.

View grouped notifications

When you receive multiple notifications from the same source, then these will appear as a "stack" of notifications on the Lock Screen. By tapping on this stack, you can expand it. You can also swipe across a group of notifications to manage them, view them or clear them all away.

Configure notifications

If you receive an unwanted notification from an app or person, then you can customize how any further notifications from this source will appear. To do this, **swipe the notification to the left** then tap the Manage button. A panel will slide up from the bottom of the screen, with two large buttons: Deliver Quietly, and Turn Off...

- **Delivery Quietly**
  Press **Deliver Quietly,** and any further notifications from this source will only appear inside Notification Center, so you won't see any more Lock Screen notifications from this source, banners, app icon badges, or hear any sounds.

- **Turn Off**
  Press **Turn Off**, and you'll switch off all future notifications.

  If you want to adjust notifications with more detail, then there's a **Settings** button at the bottom of the panel.

The Basics

Talk to Siri

Take command of your very own assistant...

Imagine Siri as your very own personal assistant. He (or she depending on your country of origin) can make calls for you, dictate emails and messages, make a restaurant reservation, remind you to do things, tell you about movies, make jokes, and much more.

Siri isn't perfect, however. It can't remember interactions from the past, it relies on hearing your voice in a clear manner, and it needs a connection to the internet to work. If you're aware of these limitations and don't mind the odd false request, then Siri can save time and even be a little fun to use.

Activate Siri

To enable Siri just hold down on the **Power** button. After two seconds you'll hear Siri chime. You can now begin issuing commands, or if you're unsure, stay quiet and after a moment or two you'll see some of the things you can ask Siri.

Speak to Siri

Say out loud, "*What's the weather like today?*" Siri will automatically look for a weather report then tell you what it's going to be like. It's that simple to use Siri. When you're finished with Siri, press the **Power** button to return to where you were before.

Dictate text with Siri

If you'd like Siri to dictate a message or email, then simply say something like, "*Tell Noah I'll be late*". Siri will automatically create a new message or email to the recipient that says 'I'll be late home tonight'.

Activate Siri via voice command

It's possible to activate Siri by simply saying "*Hey Siri.*" After you hear the recognizable Siri chime, say a command out loud (such as "tell me the time") and Siri will respond – all without your touch. To enable this feature, go to **Settings > Siri & Search**, and turn on **Listen for "Hey Siri"**.

Things you can ask Siri...

"Play something by Monsters and Men"

"Remind me to call Michael at 7."

"Set up a meeting with Sarah at 9."

"Send a message to Dave"

"Email Chris to say I'm running late."

"Show me movies directed by Steven Spielberg"

"What is the Microsoft stock price?"

"How do I get to Tom's?"

"Do I look fat in this?"

"What are your best chat-up lines?"

"What's 15 plus 26 plus 12 plus 4?"

"Roll the dice." or "Flip a coin."

"Schedule a haircut on Tuesday at 1 p.m."

The Basics

Accounts, emails, and passwords

Learn how to add your email account, calendar events, and passwords...

As you use your iPhone to do day to day things, such as checking emails, adding calendar events, or logging into websites, then you're going to start accumulating login details, accounts, and passwords. On this page you'll learn the basics of adding accounts and personal details. Most of it happens automatically, and once you've added an account you'll be able to start emailing friends and family, check your calendar for events, plus much more.

Add your email account

Start by opening the **Settings** app, then tap on **Passwords & Accounts**.

Tap on **Add Account**.

Select your email provider. If your email address ends with "gmail.com", then tap on Google. If it ends with "hotmail.com", select the Outlook option. You get the idea.

Your device will ask for the username and password associated with your email account. Simply enter these and tap **Next**.

Your device will verify your mail account details. Once the process has completed you can choose whether you wish to sync mail, contacts and notes.

Chapter 2

Add calendar events you've saved to Gmail, Outlook, or a personal account

If you've ever used a Gmail or Outlook account to add calendar events, then your iPhone can automatically load these from the internet and add them to the Calendar app. Similarly, when you add a new event or modify an existing one, your iPhone will sync the changes to your account on the internet. This means if you log into your account using a web browser or another computer, all the changes you made on your iPhone will appear there too.

If you've already added your Apple, Gmail, Outlook, or Yahoo account...

1. Start by opening the **Settings** app, then tap on **Passwords & Accounts**.
2. Tap on your account.
3. On the following screen, toggle the **Calendar** button on, so it appears green.

If you're adding a new account...

1. Start by opening the **Settings** app, then tap on **Passwords & Accounts**.
2. Tap on the **Add Account** option, then select your email provider from the list displayed on-screen.
3. Your iPhone will ask for the username and password associated with your email account. Simply enter these and tap **Next**.
4. Your device will verify your mail account details. Once the process has completed you can choose whether you wish to sync mail, contacts and notes.

Look for a password

Whenever you login into a website and enter a username, email address, or password, your iPhone will ask if you would like to save these details on the device. If you agree, the next time you go back to the website and try to log in, your iPhone will automatically offer to enter your details. It's a great time-saving feature, and it also means you don't have to remember every single password you've ever entered.

Sometimes you might need to take a look at these passwords and login details. Perhaps you're using someone else's computer and can't remember your password, or maybe you've accidentally saved multiple login details for a site and want to tidy them up. Here's how you can access every password and account saved on your iPhone in a few steps...

1. Open the **Settings** app, then tap on **Passwords and Accounts**. At the top of the screen, choose **Website & App Passwords**.
2. Your iPhone will automatically scan your face, to make sure it's you that's accessing your personal details.
3. You'll then see a list of every website you've ever logged into.
4. You can search for a website, username, email address, or password, by using the search field at the top of the screen.
5. You can also tap on individual accounts to see the details you've saved.
6. To delete a set of details, swipe across the account from right to left, then tap the red **Delete** button.

The Basics

Type like a Pro

Become a master at typing on the iPhone keyboard...

The software keyboard built into your iPhone is amazing in several ways. It guesses what word you're trying to write, then automatically finishes it for you. It rotates with the screen to make typing easier. It can even detect up to 10 fingertips to make typing quicker. If you're new to typing on a glass screen then give it some time. The first few days might be frustrating as you work out how best to hold your iPhone. Personally, I like to hold my iPhone in both hands, and use my thumbs to type each key, but everyone has their own way of typing on a screen. To get you started, here are some tips for making the most out of the iPhone's keyboard...

Cap locks

You can enable cap locks by tapping the **Shift** key once, but if you quickly double-tap the caps lock key, it will stay enabled. That means you can easily WRITE FULL SENTENCES IN CAPITAL LETTERS.

Slide to type numbers

You can easily add a number by holding your finger on the 123 key, then sliding it to a number that appears. This slide-to-type method also works with capital letters.

Create your own shortcuts

With shortcuts enabled, you can type "omw" and your iPhone will automatically write "On my way!" To create your own shortcuts go to **Settings > General > Keyboard > Text Replacement**.

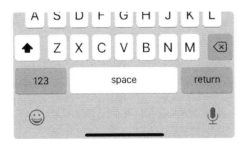

Use Emojis

You can quickly include an emoji with a message by tapping the Emoji button in the bottom-left corner of the keyboard.

Include a Memoji Sticker

You can also include your very own personalized Memoji sticker with a message. Just tap the **Memoji** button above the keyboard. To learn how to create your own Memoji, jump to the Messages chapter on page 76.

Predictive Text

Predictive Text attempts to guess the next word you want to type. To see it in action, open the **Messages** app and begin to reply to a recipient. As you enter each letter, a series of words will appear above the keyboard. To use a word just tap on it.

Chapter 2

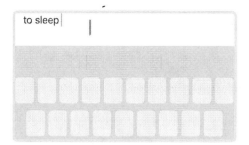

Easily move the text cursor

If you'd like to quickly move the text cursor to another word or line **tap and hold** on the spacebar then use it as a trackpad with your finger.

Accents and extra keys

To add accents, extra letters and punctuation, **tap and hold** on a key. You'll see extra options and letters appear above your finger. To select one, simply drag your finger to it then let go.

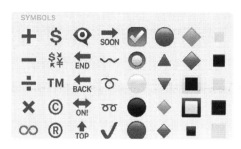

Add a trademark symbol

To find the trademark, copyright and registered symbols, open the **Emoji** keyboard then tap the character button that's second from the right. Swipe through the emojis a few times and eventually you'll see the trademark, copyright and registered symbols.

Use swipe to type

If you'd rather write words by swiping from one letter to another, then you can do just this using the keyboard on your iPhone. Here's how it works:

1. Instead of tapping each key, place your finger on the first letter in a word, then swipe it to the next letter.

2. Keep on swiping from letter to letter until you've completed the word, then lift your finger.

3. There's no need to tap the spacebar, just start swiping the next word, and your iPhone will automatically enter a space.

With practice, you might find swiping to type even quicker than tapping each key, but keep in mind that you might make a few mistakes when you first try swiping. Like typing with two thumbs, swiping to type is a skill which takes time to master.

The Basics

How to cut, copy and paste

Discover how to copy something then paste it somewhere else...

Copying and pasting is a great way to move text or content from one app to another. For example, you could copy your address from Contacts and paste it into Safari, or copy a photo and then paste it into an email. The options are endless.

Copy and paste gestures

It takes some practice, but the best way to copy and paste text is to use a series of three-finger gesures. Start by selecting a piece of text (to do this just tap and hold on the text), then perform one of the following gestures:

- **Copy**: Perform a three-finger pinch.
- **Cut**: Three-finger double pinch.
- **Paste**: Three-finger pinch out.
- **Undo**: Swipe left with three fingers.
- **Redo**: Swipe right with three fingers.
- **Access a shortcut menu:** Three-finger tap.

When you successfully use one of the three-finger gestures you'll see a confirmation at the top of your screen. Here's how it looks:

Chapter 2

Copy text without a gesture

Find a source of text on your iPhone, perhaps your phone number in Contacts. **Tap and hold** your finger on the number, let go when the magnifying glass appears, then choose **Copy** from the pop-up button.

Paste text without a gesture

Next, close Contacts and open the Notes app. Create a new note by tapping the **plus** icon, then **tap and hold** on the empty note and choose **Paste**. Your phone number will appear in the new note.

Copy images

To copy an image from the Photos app, open it, tap the **Share** button in the bottom corner, then choose **Copy**. You can now paste this image into a new email, SMS or iMessage.

Cursor navigation

You can pick up the cursor and drag it somewhere else.

Multiselect text

Quickly select a block of text by dragging your finger across it.

Intelligent text selection

You can select a word with a double tap, a sentence with three taps, and a whole paragraph with four taps.

69

The Basics

How to use the Share sheet

Learn how to share something with other people or perform actions...

There's a lot you can do with a photo on your iPhone. You can edit it (which we cover in the Photos chapter), share it with friends, hide it, duplicate it, print it, save it to the Files app, or even create a watch face on your Apple Watch. The same goes for other things on your iPhone, like notes, reminders, and web pages. You can share all of these things (and more) by using the Share sheet, which you can access by pressing the Share button. It's usually tucked away in a corner, and it looks like this:

Share something with a friend

When you tap the Share button, you'll see contact suggestions near the top of the panel. These are based on your recent activity with friends and family, so you might see a shortcut to email something, attach it to a message or AirDrop it from one Apple device to another.

App shortcuts

Below the contact suggestions panel are a series of app shortcuts. If you decide to share a photo, you might see shortcuts for sending it within a message, posting it on Facebook, or attaching it within a note.

Other shortcuts

Scroll down the Share sheet, and you'll find a wide range of context-sensitive shortcuts. These are based on the thing you're sharing, so if it's a photo, you'll see shortcuts to hide it, duplicate it, or even make a watch face for your Apple Watch. Decide to share a web page, and you'll see shortcuts for adding a bookmark, finding a piece of on-page text and copying the URL.

Chapter 2

Use AirDrop to share files

Send photos or files to friends nearby...

Have you ever wanted to share a photo, note, or video with someone else in the same room? So long as they also have an iPhone, iPad, or Mac, then it's possible to wirelessly transfer something with just a few taps. It works using a combination of Wi-Fi and Bluetooth, and there's no setup required. As a result it's never been quicker or easier to share files with friends, family and colleagues.

Enable AirDrop

To turn on AirDrop go to **Settings** > **General** > **AirDrop**. You can also use Control Center. To do this open Control Center, tap and hold on the box in the top-left corner, then tap **AirDrop**.

Share a file

AirDrop is now active. To share a file, open a photo, note, web page, or anything else with share capabilities, then tap the blue **Share** button at the bottom of the screen. You'll see the AirDrop button near the middle of the Share sheet. Tap this and you'll see anyone nearby with AirDrop enabled. To share the file with them, just tap on their face or name.

Choose who to share files with

By default, only people saved in your Contacts book can share files with you. To change this setting and let anyone send you a file:

1. Open Control Center.
2. Tap and hold on the top-left box.
3. Tap the **AirDrop** button.
4. Choose whether anyone can send you files, just your Contacts, or turn AirDrop off.

The Basics

Data Roaming & Personal Hotspots

Learn about data roaming, personal hotspots and more

Worrying about data usage and cost is a real problem for millions of iPhone users, especially when network carriers bury hidden fees for things such as using your phone abroad. Open the Settings app, select the Mobile Data option and you'll find a series of toggle switches for enabling Data Roaming, Wi-Fi calling and much more.

Data Roaming

So you're going on vacation and (obviously) you want to take your iPhone with you to browse the web, check the weather and stay in touch with loved ones. Depending on where you're going there's a chance you might be hit with fees once you return home. That's because when you stray out of your home country, your phone will piggyback onto another networks connection. Depending on the network, costs for making calls and using the web might be different to what you pay at home. This is called Data Roaming. Typically:

- **If you're travelling internationally:** Your network will charge you extra to make calls and use the internet (AKA Data Roaming).

- **Travelling within the EU:** If you're European and you're going from one EU country to another, then it's totally free to use your phone for calls and the internet.

Avoid roaming chargers

To quickly turn off roaming chargers, go to **Settings** > **Mobile Data** > **Mobile Data Options**, and toggle **Data Roaming** off.

Chapter 2

Toggle Wi-Fi calling

If the signal is pretty bad, or you want to save on precious minutes, then it's possible to enable Wi-Fi calling on your iPhone, which basically uses a local Wi-Fi signal to transmit calls digitally across the web. To enable this:

1. Open the **Settings** app.

2. Tap **Mobile Data**.

3. Tap **Wi-Fi Calling**.

4. Toggle **Wi-Fi Calling on This iPhone** on.

From this panel you can also toggle a switch which lets your iPad, Mac and Apple Watch make Wi-Fi calls. It does this by using your iCloud account for authentication, rather than your iPhone, which means your iPhone doesn't need to be nearby to make calls.

Use a Personal Hotspot to share your phone's connection

If you don't have access to a Wi-Fi network and want to share your iPhone's connection with an iPad, Mac, or another phone, then go to **Settings > Personal Hotspot** and toggle it on. You can also set a password from this panel.

Next, open the other device, go to the Wi-Fi connection screen and look for your iPhone. Select it, enter the password and you're good to go.

Keep in mind that using your iPhone as a personal hotspot can quickly drain battery. That's because your iPhone is both receiving and transmitting data at the same time.

The Basics

Use Handoff to work between devices

Start something on your iPhone then continue it on your iPad or Mac...

Most people won't have heard about Handoff. It's a rather clever feature which lets you start something on your iPhone, then continue it on an iPad or Mac.

Take writing an email for example, you might begin to compose a message on your iPhone, then sit down at your desk and finish the email on your Mac. Or maybe you start reading a web page on your iPhone then continue it on an iPad with a bigger screen. Here's how it works:

Turn Handoff on

To enable Handoff on your iPhone, go to **Settings** > **General** > **Handoff**, then toggle the **Handoff** switch on.

On a Mac, open **System Preferences**, click **General**, then ensure **Allow Handoff between this Mac and your iCloud devices** is ticked.

Jump from iPhone to Mac

It's easy to swap tasks between an iPhone and Mac. Take reading a web page for example. When you open a web page on your iPhone, a Safari icon will appear on the left-side of the Dock on the Mac. Just click on this icon to open the same webpage on your Mac.

This same process goes for composing Notes, Emails and Messages, or adding Calendar and Contact entries.

Jump from iPhone to iPad

If you'd like to continue a task on your iPad, begin writing, adding, or reading content on your iPhone, then turn on your iPad and go to the Home screen. You'll see an icon on the right-side of the Dock for the relevant app, with a small iPhone above it. Tap on this icon and you'll open the content from your iPhone, on your iPad.

Requirements

Handoff requires a Mac running Yosemite or later to talk to your iPhone, so you'll need a 2012 iMac or later, MacBook Air, MacBook Pro, or late 2013 Mac Pro. Additionally, you'll need to have Bluetooth enabled on every device, and they all need to be approximately 30 feet or less from each other.

Chapter 2

Emergency SOS

How to quickly call the emergency services or disable Face ID...

If the worst ever happens and you need to call emergency services, just press the **Power** buttons **five** times to enable Emergency SOS mode

When activated you can quickly show your medical ID card or call the emergency services. The Face ID sensor is also deactivated, preventing someone from unlocking your device with your face.

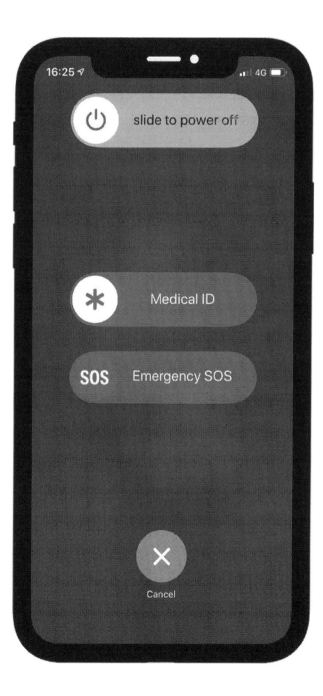

Automatically call the emergency services

If you'd like to automatically call the emergency services whenever SOS mode is activated go to **Settings > Emergency SOS** and toggle **Auto Call** on. Now, when you activate Emergency SOS mode a countdown will begin, accompanied by a warning tsound, before your iPhone automatically calls the emergency services.

Set up Emergency Contacts

If you would like to notify contacts with an automated message whenever Emergency SOS mode is activated, open the **Health** app, tap **Medical ID** then tap the **Edit** button in the top-right corner of the screen. In the slide-up panel, scroll down, tap add emergency contact and choose someone from your Contacts book.

The Basics

Use Apple Pay to buy things

Leave your wallet at home...

For those times when you don't want to carry a wallet around, Apple Pay can be pretty helpful. You can use it to pay for items at the checkout with your iPhone, pay for bus tickets, or buy items online using Safari. The experience is even better if you have an Apple Watch, because when you're ready to pay for something you only need to wave your wrist near the payment reader.

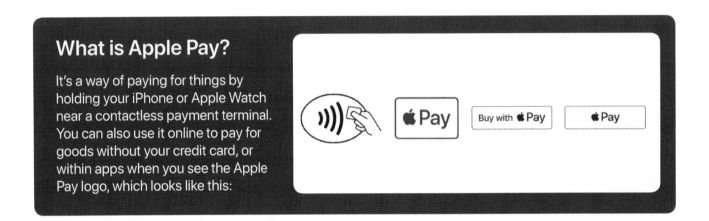

What is Apple Pay?

It's a way of paying for things by holding your iPhone or Apple Watch near a contactless payment terminal. You can also use it online to pay for goods without your credit card, or within apps when you see the Apple Pay logo, which looks like this:

How to enable Apple Pay on your iPhone

The first step is to add a credit or debit card to the Wallet app, of which you can hold a maximum of eight. Here's how:

1. Open the **Wallet** app and follow the steps to add a card. If you're asked to enter the same card used with your iTunes account, you only need to enter its security code.

2. Tap **Next** and your bank will authorize and add your card. If your bank needs more details you can add these later via **Settings** > **Wallet & Apple Pay,** then tap on your new card.

Chapter 2

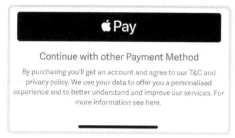

Use Apple Pay in a store

When you're ready to pay for something, just hold your iPhone near the contactless reader, then when the screen turns on look at it to use Face ID to confirm the purchase. You can also activate Apple Pay before making the purchase by pressing the **Power** button twice.

Use Apple Pay online

If you're using Safari and see the Apple Pay button at the checkout, just tap the button to make the purchase immediately.

Use Apple Pay in an app

If you're using an app and see the Apple Pay logo, you might need to toggle a setting that enables Apple Pay first — the app will let you know. Once enabled, tap the **Apple Pay** button, ensure all the details are correct, then use Face ID to confirm your identity.

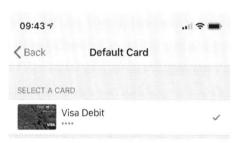

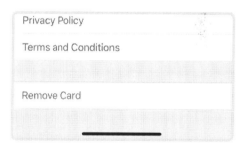

Choose which card to use

The card linked to your Apple ID will automatically be the default card for Apple Pay, but you can change the default card via **Settings > Wallet & Apple Pay > Default Card**.

See your recent transactions

Every time you use Apple Pay the last few transactions will be stored as virtual receipts on your iPhone. To see these go to **Settings > Wallet & Apple Pay**, tap on the credit/debit card of choice and any payments will appear in the **Transactions** section.

Remove a debit or credit card

Open the **Wallet** app, tap on the card you wish to remove, then tap the **Info** tab which appears near the top of the screen. Swipe down and you can remove the card by tapping **Remove Card**.

How to return an item bought using Apple Pay

If you've decided that the item you've purchased isn't right and you want to return it, then the cashier can use the last four digits of your Device Account Number to find and process the refund. To find this by go to **Settings > Wallet & Apple Pay**, then tap the card. The cashier should be able to do the rest of the work.

It's worth noting that depending on the store policies, your refund might take a few days to reappear in your bank account.

The Basics

Use AirPlay to stream content to a TV

Send video and music to your TV, or even your iPhone's entire screen...

With AirPlay you can wirelessly stream content to an Apple TV, or play music over AirPlay speakers such as HomePod. All you need to do is connect your iPhone to the same Wi-Fi connection shared with your AirPlay devices; there are no complicated configurations to set up, all the hard work is done for you.

What you can stream to an AirPlay device:

- Music and Beats 1 Radio

What you can stream to an Apple TV:

- Movies and videos
- Music and Beats 1 Radio
- Photos and slideshows
- Third-party video-based apps (such as Netflix or BBC iPlayer)
- Your entire iPhone display

Stream content to your Apple TV

1. Connect your iPhone to the same Wi-Fi connection as the Apple TV.

2. Swipe down from the top-right corner of the screen to access Control Center.

3. You will see a wireless icon in the top-right corner of the playback control window. Tap it to choose the Apple TV or AirPlay device.

4. If you've never connected your device to the Apple TV before, enter the 4-character passcode that appears on the TV.

To turn off AirPlay, return to Control Center, tap the playback controls window, tap **AirPlay** then select your device. You can also press the **Back** button on the Apple TV remote.

Chapter 2

Stream a video you're watching to an Apple TV

While watching a video tap the screen to access playback controls, then tap the **AirPlay** button. In the pop-up window, select the Apple TV and you'll start to stream the video.

Mirror your iPhone display

Want to share your iPhone screen on your Apple TV? It's easy, just swipe down from the top-right corner of the screen to access Control Center, tap **Screen Mirroring** then choose the Apple TV.

Your iPhone will immediately begin mirroring its display. While your screen is being mirrored everything you do on the iPhone will appear on-screen, including messages, websites and apps. Note how the images rotates into landscape mode when your turn your device on its side. Also note, that if you view a photo or video while mirroring it will appear full-screen on the TV. To turn off mirroring, just bring Control Center back up, tap the white **Apple TV** button, then tap **Stop Mirroring**. Alternatively, lock your iPhone via the power button and the stream will end, or if you have the Apple TV remote to hand press the **Back** button.

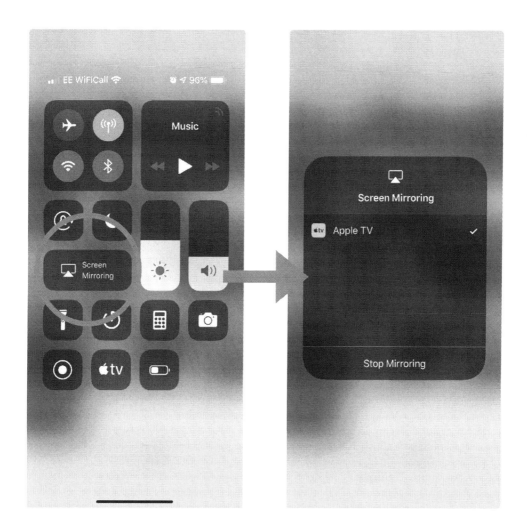

79

Web & Communication

With an iPhone in your hand, you're never out of reach from friends and loved ones. Similarly, you have the world's knowledge at your fingertips, thanks to the powerful Safari browser.

Over the next few pages, you'll learn how to browse the web on your iPhone, send messages with animated effects, send emails with attachments, block people from calling you, make a video call, plus much more.

Contents:

Use Safari to browse the web	82
Chat using Messages	86
Check your email	96
Phone tips	100
Make a FaceTime video call	102

Web and Communication

Use Safari to browse the web

Visit websites, organize tabs, customize your experience, and more...

The Safari app is the very best way to browse the web on your iPhone.

It's blazingly fast, rendering web pages in an instant. It supports Apple Pay, so you can make purchases on the web without entering your credit card details. It can strip all the ads and junk out of a page to show you only the content you want to see, it automatically blocks pop-ups, and so much more.

You'll find the Safari app already installed on your iPhone. To locate it, just unlock your iPhone then tap on this icon:

The basics of using Safari

1. Tap the **search** field to search the web or type a website address.

2. Tap the **AA** button to adjust text size, request the desktop-size version of a website, toggle Content Blockers or adjust website settings.

3. Tap this curved arrow to refresh the page. **Tap and hold** to view the desktop version of a site.

4. Use these arrows to go back a page, or forward a page.

5. Tap the **Share** button to send a webpage to another iPhone, message a link, email a link, print the page and much more.

6. Tap the **Bookmark** button to view your website bookmarks, Reading List, and browsing history.

7. Tap the **Tab** button to view all of the tabs open on your iPhone.

Chapter 3

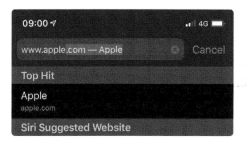

How to enter a website address

To visit a website, tap on the address field and enter an URL via the on-screen keyboard. Tap the blue **Go** button on the keyboard to visit the site.

How to search the internet

The address bar in Safari also acts as a search engine, so to search the web for any question or search term, just type your query into the address bar at the top of the screen.

Search suggestions

As you type into the address bar, notice that Safari offers search suggestions in real-time. Tap on a suggestion or the blue **Go** button on the keyboard to confirm your query.

Control panel

While browsing the web, Safari will automatically hide the control panel at the bottom of the screen. This gives web pages more room to show content and images...

Show the control panel

To quickly restore the control panel, tap anywhere along the bottom of the screen. You'll see the panel slide back into place.

Go back a page

To go back to the last page, swipe your finger from the very left side of the screen inwards. You can also go forward a page by swiping inwards from the right.

Tabs

Think of a tab as a single view of a webpage. You can have as many tabs open on your iPhone as you like, but you can only view one at a time.

Access the Tabs view

To access the tabs view, tap the **tabs** button in the very bottom right corner of the screen. It looks like two overlapping squares.

Open and close Tabs

To open a new tab view, press the **plus** button at the bottom of the screen. To close a tab, press the small **X** button in it's top-left corner.

Use Safari to browse the web

iCloud tabs

Using iCloud, tabs are automatically synced across all of your Apple devices. To access them, tap the **tabs** button, then push the tab view upwards.

Remove clutter from web pages

To remove ads and clutter from a webpage, tap the **AA** button then choose **Show Reader View**.

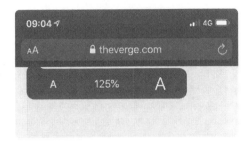

Adjust text size

If you're struggling to read small text on a page, tap the **AA** button then tap the **A** button at the top of the panel. You can keep increasing (or descreasing) until text is easy to read.

Search a web page for text

Looking for a keyword, name, or figure on a web page? By pressing the **Share** button, then tapping **Find on Page**, you can search a web page for anything text-based.

Block ads and junk from slowing down the web

Using Safari it's possible to install "extensions" which prevent adverts from loading on web pages. To install and active a content blocker, open the App Store and search for "*content blocker*". Once you've chosen an app install it then go to **Settings > Safari > Content Blockers** and toggle the content blocker app "**on**".

Apple Pay

If you see the Apple Pay button at the checkout, tap it to pay for your item/s without using a credit card.

Apple Pay requires a valid credit card. If you haven't already set one up, go to **Settings > Wallet & Apple Pay > Add Credit or Debit Card** and follow the on-screen instructions.

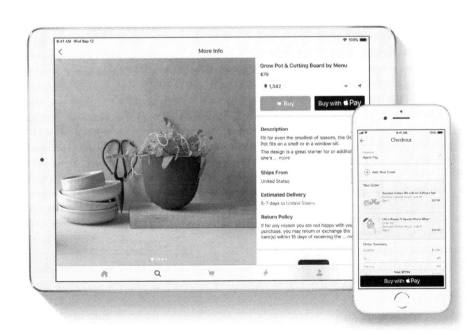

Chapter 3

Enable Private Browsing

You can browse the web without saving any history, searches, passwords or field entries by enabling Private Browsing mode. To do this, tap the **Tabs** button, then tap the **Private** button. You'll then notice the Safari interface change color from white to grey. To disable Private Browsing mode, re-open the **tabs** window then tap the **Private** button again.

Change the default search engine

By default, Safari searches the web using results from Google. If you'd rather search using Yahoo!, Bing, or DuckDuckGo, go to **Settings > Safari > Search Engine**.

Share a page

Sometimes it's helpful to share a website with friends and family. Safari offers a wealth of sharing options, including the ability to email web pages, send an URL via the messages app, and much more.
To access these sharing abilities, tap the **Share** icon at the bottom of the screen (it looks like a square with an arrow pointing upwards out of it). You'll see the share panel slide up the screen, with icons and shortcuts to each sharing ability. Tap on whichever is most suitable for your needs.

 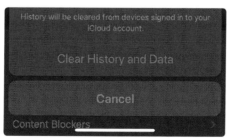 

Quickly type domain addresses

There's no need to manually type .com, .co.uk or .net. Instead, touch and hold the **full-stop key** on the keyboard to choose from a variety of .com and other suffixes.

Clear your web browsing history

If you need to clear your browsing history, go to **Settings > Safari** then tap the **Clear History** button.

Save a webpage as a PDF

To save a website as a PDF on your iPhone, visit the web page you wish to save, tap the **Share** button, then choose **Markup**. You can then annotate the webpage before saving it as a PDF in iCloud or the Files app.

85

Web and Communication

Chat using Messages

Send messages, photos, emojis, and even animated faces...

Messages is the most commonly used app for iPhone, which perhaps isn't surprising when you consider that more than 2 billion iMessages are sent each day.

In case you've been living under a rock, the Messages app is used to send text messages from one phone to another. But there's so much more. It's also possible to message iPads and Macs, send videos, drawings, animated messages, and even see the location of friends. The Messages app might initially look simple to use, but it's a surprisingly complex and versatile app. To find it, just look for the green app icon with a speech bubble:

The basics of using Messages

1. Tap the **back arrow** to return to the main Messages panel at any point.

2. Tap on a persons name or image to see more details about them.

3. Tap the **Camera** button to take a photo on the spot, or tap the **Photos** button to send an image from your library.

4. Tap and hold the **Microphone** button to send an audio message. Let go when you've finished recording.

5. Access a variety of characterful emojis by tapping this button.

6. If you need to move the cursor around, tap and hold on the **spacebar** to turn the keyboard into a trackpad.

Chapter 3

What's an iMessage...

This is a message sent directly from one Apple device to another. iMessages are sent completely free, are automatically encrypted between devices (so no one can read them), can be sent over a Wi-Fi network, and can contain video content, photos, audio, and maps. There's also no character or size limit, so your messages can be as long or as complicated as you like. iMessages always appear as blue bubbles in the chat window, while regular SMS messages appear green.

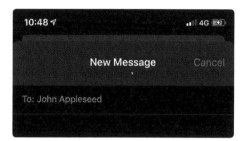

How to send a new message

From the home panel of the Messages app, tap the **New Message** icon in the top-right corner of the screen. In the **To**: field, begin to type the name of a contact, their email address or a phone number. If the contact already exists on your iPhone then you'll see their name appear above the keyboard. You can tap on this entry to automatically fill the To: field, or continue to enter the recipient's details until complete.

Send a message

Once you've entered a recipients contact details, tap the text entry field just above the keyboard, then type a message. Once you're ready to send, tap the **blue arrow** button (sometimes it's green if the other person doesn't have an iPhone), above the keyboard and the message will be sent.

Explore the App Drawer

The app drawer within the Messages app lets you do incredible things like share your travel plans, discover a song using Shazam, send stickers, and more.

To find it, look above the keyboard and you'll find the App Drawer. Tap on an app icon to use it, or tap the **App Store** icon to discover more apps.

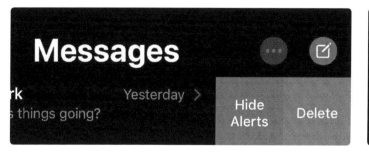

Delete a conversation

There are two ways to remove chat conversations from the Messages app. The simplest is to **swipe right-to-left** across the chat conversation from the home page of the Messages app. Alternatively, tap the **Edit** button at the top of the Messages screen, select the conversation/s that you wish to delete, then tap the **Delete** button.

See when a message was sent

Here's a great tip that goes unnoticed by most: to see the exact time a message was sent or received, **slide the chat window to the left** using your finger. You'll see the chat bubbles slide to one side and the time each was sent/received appear.

Chat using Messages

Create your very own Memoji

Sending a video message of your face is so 2017, because with the new Memoji feature, you can now create your very own 3D avatar, then use it to send fun animated messages to friends and family. Here's how it works:

1. Open the **Messages** app, then tap on the **Animoji** button. It looks like a monkeys face.

2. Tap the **+** button to create a custom Memoji. Scroll to the left if you don't see it.

3. Use the creation tool to create your very own Memoji.

4. Tap **Done** in the top-right corner to save and use your new Memoji.

Let's take a more detailed look at some of the Memoji options available:

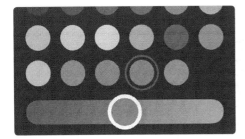

Skin colors

Memojis start life with yellow skin, but you're given 17 other colors to choose from including green, blue, or purple.

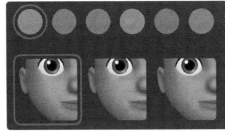

Freckles, cheeks & beauty spots

While choosing a skin color, you can also choose from three types of freckles, four cheek blushes, and six beauty spot placements.

Hairstyle

There's a wealth of hairstyles to choose from, and each can be customized with highlights or unique colors.

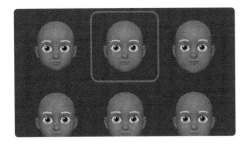

Head shape

Choose from a selection of head shapes. There are also three different ages to select.

Eyes, eyelashes and brows

Select from 9 eye shapes, 9 eyelash designs, and 15 types of eyebrow.

Nose and Lips

Whatever shape nose you have, you'll find the corresponding shape here in the Memoji creator. You can also pick from a range of lip shapes, colors and piercings.

Chapter 3

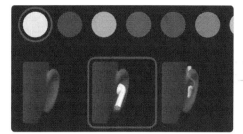

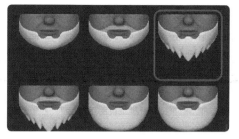

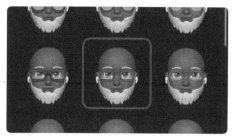

Ears

The Memoji creator includes a large selection of ear types to choose from. You can also add earrings and studs – or even a pair of Airpods.

Facial Hair

The Memoji creator comes with 3 types of facial hair: moustache, beard, and sideburn. There are dozens to choose from, and of course, they can each be customized using color.

Eyewear

Whether you wear glasses or sunglasses, you'll find a large amount of eyewear types to choose from. You can even change the lens color using a secondary control.

Replace your head with an Memoji or Animoji

If you want to really surprise someone, then sending a photo or video of yourself with your face replaced with an Memoji, is a good way to do that. What's particularly impressive is that the Memoji matches your head movements perfectly. There's even a subtle shadow below to make it look almost realistic. Here's how it works:

1. Tap the **Camera** icon to the left of the message field.
2. Tap the **Effects** button in the bottom-left corner.
3. Tap the **Animoji** button.
4. Choose a Memoji.
5. Press the small **X** button to close the Animoji panel.
6. Pose, then take a photo.
7. Press the **white/blue** button to send your snap.

Chat using Messages

Send an Animoji

Using the Messages app you can create and send animated emojis using your face. Animojis track more than 50 facial movements and can be used to create amazing animated expressions. To create and send an Animoji:

1. When you're viewing or replying to a message, tap the **Animoji** icon. It looks like a monkeys face.

2. You'll immediately see the Animoji come to life on the screen as it mirrors your facial expressions and head movements.

3. To navigate through the different Animojis, slide the panel of faces sideways. To see all of them at once, slide the Animoji panel upwards.

4. Tap the **record** button, and the Animoji will start recording. Say your message out-loud and play around with expressions.

5. After you're done, tap the **record** button to end. You'll see a preview of the recording. To send the Animoji, just tap the blue **Send** button.

Send an emoji

Emoji's are awesome. Each one is a beautifully designed graphic that represents a word, emotion or object, and by mixing emoji's with words you can really add emotion or humor to a message.

To send an emoji tap the **Emoji** button on the keyboard while composing a message. It's at the bottom of the screen next to the spacebar and microphone. You can swipe left and right to scroll through emoji's or tap the grey icons at the bottom of the screen to jump to an emoji category.

Chapter 3

Add a camera effect or filter to a photo

If you want to add a filter to a photo, a caption, make an annotation, or add a cool effect, then here's how:

1 Tap the **Camera** icon to the left of the message field.

2 Take a photo or video.

3 Tap the **Effects** button in the bottom-left corner.

4 Use the **Effects**, **Edit**, or **Markup** buttons to add effects to your photo or video.

5 Press the **white/blue** send button to send the photo or video.

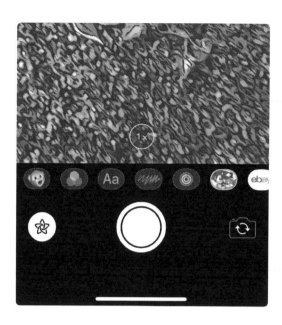

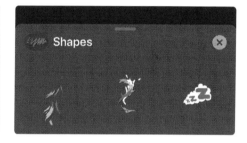

To add a filter to a photo:

Tap on the **Effects** button, tap on **Filters**, then tap on a filter to preview it. You can slide the panel upwards to see all 16 filters.

To add text or speech bubbles:

Tap on **Text**, then swipe the panel upwards to see all 18 variations. When you've made a selection you can enter your own text by typing with the keyboard, move the text box around or re-size it with two fingers.

To add a shape:

Tap on the **Effects** button, **Shapes**, then chose from one of the 23 shapes. You can also adjust the size of these or move them with your fingers.

To send a Memoji sticker:

Tap on the **Memoji** button to attach a fun sticker to your photo. To add some humor, try resizing a Memoji sticker to replace your own head.

To add an Activity sticker:

Tap on the **Activity** button to discover 29 animated fitness-themed stickers.

To add an Emoji sticker:

Scroll all the way to the right then tap on the **Emoji Stickers** button, where you'll find 19 animated emoji stickers.

Chat using Messages

Automatically turn words into emoji's

So you've composed a message, but you want to liven it up with some fun emoji's. It's surprisingly easy, thanks to a clever feature that automatically scans your message for emoji-related words then lets you replace. Here's how:

1. Compose a message with some emoji-friendly words (such as "happy", "fireworks", "pizza" etc).

2. Tap the **emoji** button on the keyboard. Any emoji-friendly words will glow gold.

3. Tap on the gold words that you'd like to replace and they will automatically swap from text to emoji graphics.

Send a Digital Touch drawing

With the Messages app you can draw a message and send it with just a few taps of your finger. Here's how it works:

1. When you're viewing or replying to a message, tap the **Digital Touch** button in the App Store panel. It looks like two fingertips over a heart.

2. Start to draw on the black panel in the bottom half of the screen. You'll see your drawing come to life.

3. Once you've finished tap the **blue arrow** icon to send the drawing.

It's not just a drawing you can send, there are five other effects including a heart beat and a fireball:

Taps

Simply tap anywhere on the black panel and an animated tap will appear.

Fireball

Press and hold on the screen with your finger. When you let go a fireball effect will be sent.

Kiss

Tap with two fingers and you'll send a kiss message.

Heartbeat

Tap and hold on the screen and an animated heartbeat will be sent.

Broken Heart

Tap and hold with two fingers then slide downwards to send a broken heart.

Chapter 3

Send a message with an animated effect

If you'd like to emphasize a message with an animated effect then four hidden effects are included within the Messages app: a slam dunk, a loud shout, gentle whisper, or invisible ink – where the recipient must swipe their finger across the message to reveal it. Here's how it works:

1. Compose your text, then instead of tapping the blue send arrow, **tap and hold** on it.
2. In the pop-up window, tap one of the four options on the right-side of the screen to see a preview of how it looks.
3. Once you're happy with an effect, tap the **blue arrow** to send the message.

Add a Tapback sticker

If you want to add a personal touch to a delivered message just **tap and hold** on the message bubble to see six stickers that can be attached and seen by the recipient.

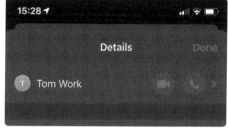

To see the details of a contact

Tap on their **name** or **image** at the top of the screen then choose **Info**. On the following panel, tap on the **small arrow** at the top of the screen to see the recipients details.

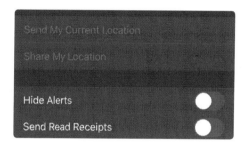

Share your current location

Meeting a friend somewhere in town? If they're having trouble finding you, tap on their **name** at the top of the screen, choose **Info**, then tap the **Send My Current Location** button.

Search for people, photos & more

From the home screen of the Messages app, pull the screen down to reveal a search bar. Tap on this and you'll be able find recent contacts, links, photos and search through message content.

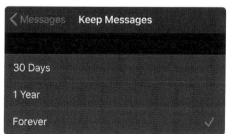

Automatically delete messages

You can tell Messages to automatically remove chats after either 30 days or 1 year. To activate this feature, go to **Settings > Messages > Keep Messages**.

Keep audio messages

By default, audio messages are automatically deleted after 2 minutes. To keep them forever, go to **Settings > Messages**, then scroll down where you'll see an option for storing audio messages for longer.

Chat using Messages

Send a full-screen effect with your message

Want to really grab someone's attention with a message? Try sending a full-screen effect. With the Messages app you can include one of nine effects that take over the screen for a brief moment:

Echo
Your message is repeated across the screen hundreds of times.

Spotlight
A brief spotlight appears on your message.

Balloons
A flurry of balloons floats up the screen.

Confetti
Great for celebratory messages!

Inflatable heart
A love balloon floats up the screen.

Lasers
A techno laser streaks across the screen.

Fireworks
Explosive fireworks erupt across the screen.

Shooting star
A blue shooting star flies across the screen then explodes.

Sparks
Glittering gold sparks fall down the screen.

Here's how to send a full-screen effect:

1. Compose your text, then instead of tapping the blue send arrow, **tap and hold** on it.

2. Tap the **Screen** tab at the top of the screen, then select an effect by swiping to the left with your finger.

3. Once you've found an effect tap the **blue arrow** button to send the message.

Note! Fullscreen effects do not work when the Reduce Motion setting is enabled. To disable it, go to **Settings > General > Accessibility > Reduce Motion**.

Hide alerts from a contact or thread

If you're being spammed with messages, or you just want some peace and quiet from a group conversation, then it's easy to mute them and prevent any further notifications. If you're already viewing the conversation thread, tap the **persons name** at the top of the screen, tap **Info**, then in the following panel toggle **Hide Alerts** on.

Alternatively, from the home page of Messages, slide the conversation thread to the left and tap **Hide Alerts**. When Hide Alerts is turned on you'll see a moon crescent icon next to the person or group. Now, whenever they send you a message you will not receive any notifications. You will, however, still see a red badge over the Messages app icon.

Delete a conversation

There are two ways to remove chat conversations from the Messages app. The simplest is to swipe right-to-left across the chat conversation from the home page of the Messages app. You'll see a red button marked **Delete** slide into view, just tap it to clear the conversation from your device:

Alternatively, tap the **Edit** button at the top of the Messages screen, then tap the conversation/s that you wish to **delete**. Once you've made your selection tap the blue Delete button in the bottom corner.

Web and Communication

Check your email

Compose messages, organize your inbox, and more...

Alongside the Messages app, Mail must come close to being on the most used apps on iPhone. That's because if you're serious about doing things on the web, like shopping or registering for services, then there's no way to avoid having an email address — it's a basic requirement for so many things.

Thankfully, the Mail app on your iPhone is easy to use and gets straight to the point. It's designed with a clean, white interface that helps you focus on what's important: your emails. Buttons are colored blue, and basic Multi-Touch gestures enable you to delete messages, flag them and more.

You'll find the Mail app already installed on your iPhone. To find it, just unlock your device then tap on this icon:

The basics of using Mail

1 Use this back arrow to return to the Mailboxes screen, where you can access your Drafts, Sent, Junk, and Trash mailboxes.

3 Looking for a particular email or recipient? Use the search box to quickly find it.

5 Tap this button to create a new email.

2 Tap **Edit** and you can select multiple emails at once. This is helpful for deleting or moving multiple messages at once.

4 This filter button in the bottom corner will display your unread emails.

Chapter 3

Quickly format text in an email

If you'd like to bold, italicize or underline a word or sentence, highlight the text then tap on the **option** arrow. Next, tap **BIU** and select the format you wish to use.

Attach images and videos

To attach an image within an email, tap and hold where you want it to go then tap the **image** button above the keyboard. There's also a camera button for taking a photo on the spot.

Attach a file from iCloud

To attach a document, PDF, zip file or image saved in iCloud, tap on the **document** button above the keyboard.

Scan and attach a document

When composing an email, it's possible to scan letters and documents, then attach them directly to a message. What's great is that scans actually look like scanned documents, thanks to some clever post-processing which straightens the image and fixes any white balance issues. To scan a document:

When composting an email, tap the **scan** button above the keyboard.

When the camera view appears, move it over the document you wish to scan and your iPhone will automatically recognize it.

Take a photo, then adjust the corners of the scan to match the document.

Tap **Keep Scan** to save the image. You can continue to scan further documents, or tap **Save** to attach the image/s to your email.

The scan will now be attached to your email as an image.

Check your email

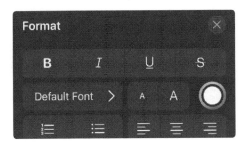

Format text

While composing an email, tap the Aa button above the keyboard to access a wide range of text editing tools, such as font family, color and layout.

Delete multiple emails

While viewing your inbox, tap the blue **Edit** text in the top right corner. Next, tap on the messages you'd like to delete, you can select as many as needed. Once you're happy with the selection, tap the **Delete** button in the bottom-right corner.

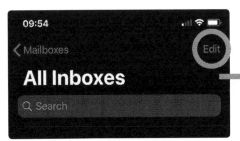

Move or mark multiple emails

Follow the steps above, but instead of deleting the selected messages select either **Mark** or **Move** at the bottom of the screen. Mark enables you to flag the messages, mark them as unread or move them to the Junk folder. Move enables you to store the emails in a separate folder from the Inbox.

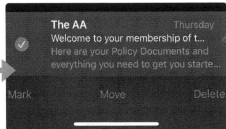

See contact details

While reading an email, tap on the name of the contact at the top of the message and you'll see their details in full.

Get email reply notifications

Waiting for an important reply to an email? You can receive a notification when it arrives by opening the email message, tapping the **arrow** button in the bottom corner, then tap **Notify Me...**

Save a contact to your device

If you'd like to save an emails contact details to your iPhone, then tap on their **name** while reading an email then select either **Create New Contact** or **Add to Existing Contact.**

Mark an email as Unread

Sometimes it's helpful to mark emails as unread so they can be later re-read or referenced. To do this just swipe the message to the right then choose **Unread**.

Chapter 3

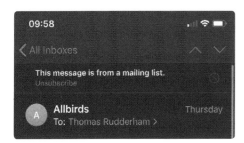

Automatically unsubscribe

If you recieve an unsolicitated marketing email and want to quickly unsubscribe, open the message then tap the **Unsubscribe** text at the top of the screen.

Forward an email

To quickly forward an email to someone else, tap the **arrow** button in the bottom-right corner, then tap **Forward**.

Print an email

To print an email, tap the **forward arrow** button at the bottom of the screen then tap **Print**. Select a wireless printer then tap **Print**.

Attach a drawing

You can attach a drawing to an email by tapping the pencil button above the keyboard (if you don't see it tap the arrow to the right). While drawing, you can choose from a variety of tools, such as a pencil, felt tip, marker, or ruler. You can further customize a tool by tapping on it, so tap on the felt tip tool and you'll be able to adjust the line thickness and opacity.

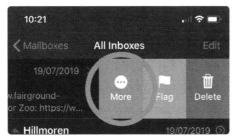

Delete an email with a swipe

Erasing emails can become a chore, so to speed up the process, simply **swipe your finger right-to-left** across the email message while in the Inbox.

More email options

After swiping an email from right-to-left, tap the **More** button and you'll see a selection of controls slide up from the bottom of the screen. Options include Reply, Forward, Mark, Notify, and Move.

Save a draft email

If you're composing an email and you're not ready to send it yet, drag the email down to the bottom of the screen. It'll stay there, below the rest of your emails, until you tap on it to continue the draft.

Web and Communication

Phone tips

Let's take a look at some phone-related tips...

The iPhone might include the word "phone" in its name, but that doesn't mean it's used primarily as a telephone. Instead, the majority of people use it as a fully fledged computer for sharing media, browsing the web and playing games.

Nevertheless, the Phone app is still an essential feature. One that's simple to use but with a handful of useful features.

Add a photo to a contact

1. Open the **Phone** app, select a contact, then tap the **Edit** button.

2. Tap the **Add Photo** button below the large grey circle.

3. You'll see options for taking a photo on the spot, or choosing one from your library, or creating your own original Animoji/Memoji. Select whichever is relevant, then scale and position the image so that the contact's face is in the center of the preview panel.

   Once you're happy with the image, tap **Done** to assign the photo to the contact.

Dial a number using Siri

If you'd rather dictate a number than tap each key, open Siri by holding the **Power** button, then say "*Call...*" followed by the number or contact name. Siri will then dial the contact automatically.

Turn off Data Roaming

When traveling abroad your phone will piggy-back on a local carrier to enable you to make download data, such as videos, social media, or the internet. This often means that you have to pay extra for each megabyte of data used, and the prices can be pretty high. To prevent a shock when the next bill arrives, go to **Settings > Mobile Data > Mobile Data Options**, and de-toggle the **Data Roaming** switch.

Chapter 3

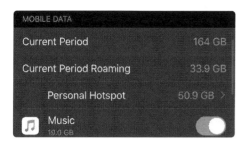

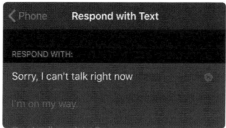

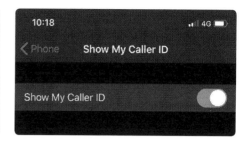

See your mobile data usage

Most network carriers limit your data usage each month. To see your current usage, go to **Settings > Mobile Data** and scroll down to the **MOBILE DATA** panel.

Respond to calls with messages

Too busy to take a call? If so it's possible to answer calls with a pre-set text message. To do this, go to **Settings > Phone > Respond with Text**.

Turn off your caller ID

If you'd like to remain anonymous when making a call, go to **Settings > Phone > Show My Caller ID** then de-toggle the switch.

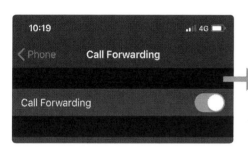

Forward calls to another number

To forward all incoming calls to another number, go to **Settings > Phone > Call Forwarding**, then toggle the switch **on**. In the following panel you can enter the number you wish calls to transfer too. When Call Forwarding is enabled you'll see the forwarding icon appear in the menu bar next to the signal strength.

Block numbers

To block a number from calling you, open the **Phone** app, tap **Recents** then tap the small **info** icon next to the number you wish to block. In the following panel tap **Block this Caller**.

Assign a custom ringtone to a contact

Assigning a custom ringtone to a contact is one of the easiest ways to instantly tell who's trying to get in touch, and it's possible to select from a variety of custom tones, as well as purchase and download ringtones based upon the latest music charts.

1 Begin by opening the **Phone** or **Contacts** app, then select the contact you'd like to assign a custom ringtone.

2 Tap the blue **Edit** button in the top-right corner of the screen, then tap the **Ringtone** button. You can now choose from a wide selection of audio tones that suit the particular contact.

3 If you prefer the older ringtones that were introduced with the very first iPhone, tap the **Classic** button at the bottom of the ringtones list. On the following panel you can select a classic tone from years gone by.

4 If you'd like to assign a music track as a tone, tap the **Tones Store** button at the top of the Ringtone screen. You'll then be taken to the Tones section of the iTunes Store.

Web and Communication

Make a FaceTime video call

Make a free video call to friends and family using FaceTime...

With FaceTime, you can be with friends and family at any time and place. Whether it's a birthday, anniversary, meeting or just a chat, FaceTime lets you be a part of the moment with crystal clear video and audio.

FaceTime works over Wi-Fi, and enables you to call another iPhone, iPad, iPod touch or a Mac. The recipient will receive an alert that's just like a phone call, and with just one tap of a finger, you're connected.

You'll find the FaceTime app already installed on your iPhone. To find it, just tap on this icon:

The basics of using FaceTime

1 You can move the preview image of yourself around the screen by dragging it with your finger.

2 Take a photo of the conversation using this white button.

3 Tap the **Effects** button to apply a wide range of filters, shapes, and video effects.

4 Mute your microphone using this button.

5 Flip your camera around using this button to show what's behind your iPhone.

6 End the call using this button.

Chapter 3

Make a FaceTime call

Open the FaceTime app and sign in if you haven't used it before. You'll see your contacts listed down the middle of the screen. Tap a contact to automatically begin calling them.

Call from Contacts

You can also select a contact from the **Phone** or **Contacts** app, then call them by tapping the **Facetime** button.

Delete your history

From the main FaceTime screen, tap the **Edit** button in the top-left corner, select any conversations you would like to clear, then tap the **Delete** button at the bottom of the screen.

Access additional controls

During a FaceTime call, drag the **lower panel upwards** to access additional controls, including the ability to disable your camera, or begin a chat conversation.

Add stickers and filters

While making a FaceTime call, tap the **Effects** button in the lower panel to explore a wide range of video effects.

Replace your face with a Memoji

If you really want to make someone laugh, then replacing your face with an Animoji or Memoji is a great way to do it. These animated 3D faces will match your movements, expressions, and mouth, so it really looks like you've become a real lift animated character. Here's how it works:

1. During the FaceTime call, tap the **Effects** button in the bottom-left corner.

2. Tap on the **Animoji** icon (it looks like a monkey), then select an existing avatar, or custom-made Memoji.

103

Camera and Photos

The iPhone is probably the best camera you own. Not because it has the best image quality or the highest megapixels, but because it's always with you, ready to capture a special moment then share it with everyone you know. It's also really clever. Using the iPhone, it's possible to take Burst Mode photos, which capture ten frames a second, take slow-motion videos, which capture 240 frames a second, or simply take a great picture, then tweak it with some incredibly powerful editing tools.

That's what this chapter is all about. You'll get to know the Camera app in all its glory, then discover how to edit and share your photos with friends and family. Before you know it, you'll be a budding photographer with a library of stunning images.

Contents:

Take a photo using iPhone X, XR or XS	106
Take a photo using iPhone 11 or 11 Pro	114
View and edit your Photos	122

Camera and Photos

Take a photo using iPhone X, XR or XS

Get to know the camera app and all of its features...

In the world of mobile technology, 2007 was a long time ago. It was practically the stone age, a time when people pressed physical buttons to interact with their devices. Then one sunny January morning, Steve Jobs unveiled the iPhone.

You already know what an impact it made on the mobile industry — it revolutionized how we interact with the internet and communicate with friends. But the iPhone also changed the entire camera industry. Today, it's the most popular camera in the world (according to Flickr). In fact, Apple devices are more popular than Canon and Nikon combined.

Over time, the camera app and hardware have become ever more advanced, until today it's able to recognize faces, analyze lighting conditions, record slow-motion video, and much more. As a result, the iPhone in your pocket is capable of taking truly beautiful photos.

To find the Camera app, just look for this icon:

The basics of using the Camera app

1 At top of the screen are shortcuts for toggling the flash, Live Photo effect, timer, and filters.

3 Quickly jump to a photo you've taken by tapping the thumbnail image.

5 Swap to the front-facing camera to take a selfie.

2 Tap the **1X** button to zoom to 2X (on iPhone X and XS).

4 Take a photo by tapping the large **white button**. Tap and hold to take a burst photo.

106

Chapter 4

Take a photo from the lock screen
The quickest way to open the Camera app is via the lock screen of your iPhone. To do this, just press on the **Camera** icon in the lower-right corner.

Live Photos
Whenever you take a photo, your iPhone captures a few frames before and after the shot. To view this back, just **tap and hold** on the image when viewing it in the Photos app.

Turn Live Photos off
If you don't need (or like) the Live Photo feature, then you can disable it by tapping the yellow **Live Photo** icon at the top of the camera window.

Capture using the volume buttons
It's possible to take a photo by pressing the **volume up or down** buttons on the side of your iPhone. This is especially useful for taking selfies with your arm outstretched.

Zoom even further
You can zoom even further (up to 10x digitally) by holding your finger on the **1x** button then sliding it to the right. If you're using an iPhone XR, just pinch your fingers on the screen to zoom.

Camera focus
The camera will automatically focus onto a prominent object or area of light, but if you need to manually focus the camera, just tap on the area or subject you wish to focus on.

Lock the focus and aperture
To lock the focus and aperture levels, tap and hold on an subject or area. After a second or two a flashing yellow box beneath your finger will indicate that the camera focus has been locked.

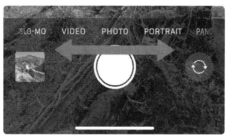

Swap camera modes
The Camera app has multiple modes, including Photo, Portrait, Video, Slow-Mo, Square and Pano. To quickly jump between them, swipe your finger either left or right across the screen.

Turn the flash on and off
To toggle the flash off, tap the lightning button in the top corner of the screen. You'll see options for activating the flash automatically, turning it on or off.

Take Amazing Photos

Take a portrait photo

Portrait photos are amazing. They mimic a DSLR camera by blurring the background behind a person. To do this your iPhone uses machine learning to automatically detect the face and hair of a subject, the distance between them and the background, then it blurs the background to create a beautiful 3D effect.

To use Portrait mode:

1. Open the **Camera** app and select **Portrait** mode.

2. Place the subject at least 2 feet away. If they are too close the Camera app will let you know.

3. Tap the **capture** button to take the photo.

Use Portrait Lighting to take amazing selfies

By using Portrait Lighting mode you can simulate a number of professional photographer effects and tools, such as a gold bounce card, to create even more beautiful looking photos. There are six effects to choose from:

Natural Light
Your subject's face in sharp focus against a blurred background.

Studio Light
A clean look with your subject's face brightly lit.

Contour Light
Adds subtle shadows and highlights to the subject's face.

Stage Light
Your subject's face is spotlit against a deep black background.

Stage Light Mono
Like Stage Light, but in black and white.

High-Key Mono
Adds a beautiful monochromatic effect.

To enable Portrait Lighting mode, open the **Camera** app and select **Portrait**. You'll see five buttons appear towards the bottom of the screen: Natural Light, Studio Light, Contour Light, Stage Light and Stage Light Mono. Select an effect by swiping through the options. Watch the screen to see the effect apply to your face in real-time. Press the **capture** button to take a photo.

You can choose another effect, even after the photo has been saved, by tapping the **Edit** button within the Photos app.

Chapter 4

Disable the Portrait mode effect

To disable the Portrait effect in a photo, open the image, tap **Edit**, then tap the yellow **Portrait** button at the top of the screen.

Shoot a video

Capturing video is easy, just swipe your finger across the camera viewfinder until the **VIDEO** is centered, then tap the **red** button.

Take a photo while filming

While filming a video, you can simultaneously capture a photo by tapping the white button below the red video button.

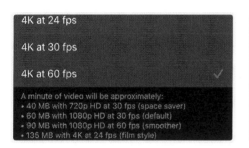

Enable 4K video recording

To enable 4K video recording, open the **Settings** app, tap **Camera**, then select **Record Video**. On the following panel you'll be able to enable video recording at 4K.

Slow motion video

One of the most fun camera features included with iPhone is the ability to shoot video in slow motion at 240 frames per second. It's great for capturing fast-moving objects.

Film in slo-mo

While in the Camera app, swipe the text at the bottom of the screen until **SLO-MO** is centered. Next, tap the red record button to start filming your slow motion video

Edit the playback speed of a slow-mo video

To edit the slow-motion parts of a video, open the video in the **Photos** app, then tap the **Edit** button.

You'll notice a timeline at the bottom of the screen that's broken up by thin white lines. In the center the lines are spaced further apart. This is the part of the clip which plays back in slow motion.

You can lengthen or shorten this slow motion part of the clip by dragging the white handles, then preview the clip by tapping the play button.

109

Take a photo using iPhone X, XR or XS

Burst mode

Action photos have typically been hard to capture on mobile devices. Whether it's someone jumping mid-air, a vehicle racing past, or a friend performing acrobatic moves, these fast-paced photos usually come out blurry or mistimed.

To make things easier, the Camera app on iPhone comes with a feature called Burst Mode. It works by taking 10 photos every second, then saves them as a collection within the Photos app. Once the collection has been saved, your iPhone automatically scans the images, then picks what it thinks is the best one. It does this by analyzing the brightness and sharpness, and by looking for faces within the image. This is then saved as a Favorite image. If it doesn't pick the right image, or if you want to save multiple snaps from a collection, then you can of course, manually pick your own favorite.

Capture a burst mode photo

When you're ready to take a burst mode photo, tap and hold the **camera** button. Let go when you've captured the moment.

Burst mode stacks

The burst mode images will now be saved as a stack within the Photos app. To see them, tap the **thumbnail** image in the bottom corner of the Camera app. You can also open the **Photos** app to see your saved photo stack.

Select a burst mode favorite

Open the stack of photos. To select a favorite, tap the **Favorites...** button at the bottom of the screen. A selection of thumbnails will appear. Scroll through them using your finger and tap on your favorite image. If you want to keep multiple images just tap on them, each will be checked with a blue tick.

Tap the **Done** button to confirm your changes. A slide-up panel will ask if you'd like to only keep your favorite/s or keep everything. Tap whichever is relevant to your needs.

How to use the Camera timer

To enable the timer, open the **Camera** app and look for a timer icon at the top of the screen. Tap it and you'll see three text options appear: **Off**, **3s** and **10s**. These correspond to the timer settings, so off is the standard setting, 3s gives you three seconds to pose, and 10s gives you 10 seconds to prepare yourself. Tap whichever you need, then tap the **Camera** button to snap a photo. You'll see a countdown appear on-screen and the camera flash will also emit a brief light for each passing second. After the countdown has ended your iPhone will quickly capture 10 photos in a second. This stack of photos will be saved in the Photos app.

To pick a favorite, open the stack and tap the blue **Select...** text. Next, swipe through the images then tap the image (or images) you wish to save. Once you're happy with the selection, tap the **Done** button.

Capture time-lapse video

Have you ever wanted to capture a sun set, the changing tides, or the movement of clouds? Using the Camera app you can do this with the time-lapse feature. It works by capturing multiple photos, instead of video, over a period of time.

To capture a time-lapse video, open the **Camera** app, then select **TIME-LAPSE**. Next, place your iPhone in a suitable location. Make sure it's steady – any movements over time will ruin the time-lapse effect. When you're ready, tap the **red record** button. Leave your iPhone for a few moments or minutes - the longer the better as you'll capture more footage - then tap the red record button again to end the time-lapse.

Take a photo using iPhone X, XR or XS

Panoramic photos

Have you ever wanted to capture an incredibly beautiful vista? By using the PANO mode you can do just this by taking a super-wide, 180-degree photo.

PANO mode works by taking one very wide continuous photo. As you rotate on the spot, the camera captures the image as it appears on the right side of the lens. If there's any movement in front of you (such as people walking by), then you might see a few visual errors, but for vistas and still scenes the PANO mode works wonders.

Capture a panoramic shot

Begin by opening the **Camera** app, then select **PANO**. You'll see a thumbnail in the center of the screen with a white arrow pointing right. Tap the **Camera** button at the bottom of the screen to start capturing a panoramic shot. Slowly pan your device to the right. Keep a steady hand — if you wobble too much black bars will appear at the top and bottom of the photo. When you've captured the scene, tap the **Camera** button again to end the shot.

Camera filters

Filters enable you to instantly alter the appearance of a photo. There are eight to choose from: Mono, Tonal, Noir, Fade, Chrome, Process, Transfer, and Instant.

Access the filters

From the main window of the **Camera** app, tap the **Filters** button in the top-right corner of the screen. It looks like three overlapped circles.

Choose a filter

You'll instantly see all eight filters previewed on the screen. Tap on one and the filter will be applied to any photos you take.

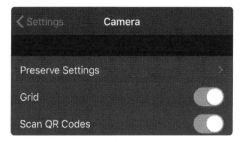 

Enable the camera grid

Taking level photos can be tricky when only using the preview window, so to help line up horizons, try enabling the camera grid. To do this, go to **Settings > Camera**, then toggle the **Grid** button on.

Next, go back to the Camera app and you'll see a 3x3 grid above the preview window.

Preserve Camera Settings

Every time you close the Camera app, then re-open it, it defaults back to the Camera mode; no matter what you were doing before. If you want to reuse a specific mode, such as the video camera, swiping back to it over and over again can be a real pain. Thankfully, there's an easy way to preserve the camera mode you were using last. Just go to **Settings > Camera > Preserve Settings** and toggle **Camera Mode** on.

Camera and Photos

Take a photo using iPhone 11 or 11 Pro

Get to know the camera app and all of its features...

There's a reason why the iPhone 11 Pro has the word "Pro" in its name: the triple-lens camera array around the back. The first lens can be used to take ultra-wide photos, the second regular photos, and the third lens has a 2x telescopic view of the world. The iPhone 11 shares two of these lenses (the ultra-wide and standard lenses), enabling both devices to take some truly beautiful images - even in the dark.

If you've purchased either an iPhone 11 or 11 Pro, then you'll notice it includes a Camera app with a different layout and set of buttons. This chapter is almost a duplicate of the previous one but focuses exclusively on the Camera app for the iPhone 11 and 11 Pro.

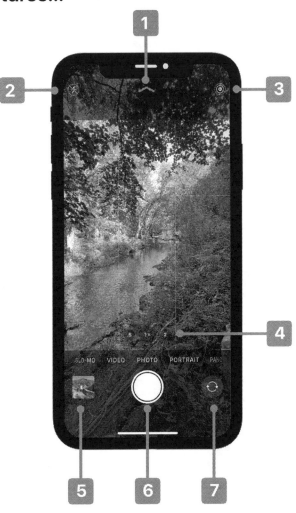

The basics of using the Camera app on the iPhone 11 and 11 Pro

1 Tap this arrow to display settings for the flash, Night Mode, Live Photo, aspect ratio, timer, and filters. They'll appear just above the shutter button.

2 Tap this icon to turn off the flash. You might also see a Night Mode toggle if you're in a dark environment.

3 Tap this icon to turn Live Photos off (so instead of seeing a brief moving image when you swipe through your photos, you'll just see a static image.

4 Tap the **.5X** button to zoom out and use the ultra-wide lens. Tap **1x** for a regular photo, or **2x** to use the telephoto lens.

5 Quickly jump to a photo you've taken by tapping the thumbnail image.

6 Take a photo by tapping the large **white button**. You can also tap and hold to record a video.

7 Swap to the front-facing camera to take a selfie.

Chapter 4

Take a photo from the lock screen

The quickest way to open the Camera app is via the lock screen of your iPhone. To do this, just press on the **Camera** icon in the lower-right corner.

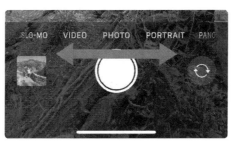

Swap camera modes

The Camera app has multiple modes, including Photo, Portrait, Video, Slow-Mo, Square and Pano. To quickly jump between them, swipe your finger either left or right across the screen.

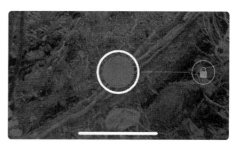

Quickly record a video

Whenever you want to quickly record a video, open the Camera app then tap and hold on the **shutter** button. To record a longer video slide your finger right towards the lock button.

Capture using the volume buttons

It's possible to take a photo by pressing the **volume up or down** buttons on the side of your iPhone. This is especially useful for taking selfies with your arm outstretched.

Zoom even further

You can zoom even further (up to 10x digitally) by holding your finger on the **1x** button then sliding it to the right.

Camera focus

The camera will automatically focus onto a prominent object or area of light, but if you need to manually focus the camera, just tap on the area or subject you wish to focus on.

Lock the focus and aperture

To lock the focus and aperture levels, tap and hold on an subject or area. After a second or two a flashing yellow box beneath your finger will indicate that the camera focus has been locked.

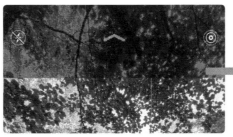
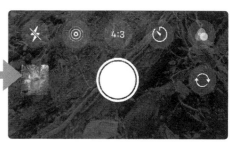

Access additional controls

Tap the **arrow** button at the top of the screen, and a series of context-sensitive controls will appear above the shutter button. For example, in Photo mode, you can adjust the aspect ratio, set a timer, or add a filter. In Night Mode, you can adjust the exposure length, and in Portrait Mode, you can adjust the aperture.

Use Night Mode to take photos in the dark

Night Mode uses a combination of the triple-lens system on the back of your iPhone, alongside some clever computational software, to capture as much light as possible in dark environments. It kicks in automatically, so often all you need to do is press the shutter button and keep your iPhone as still as possible. But if you want to adjust the exposure length, or turn Night Mode off completely, then here's what to do:

1. Open the **Camera** app and set the view to **1x** or **2x**.
2. Make sure you're in a dimly lit environment, then tap the **Night Mode** button when it appears. It'll be in the upper-right corner.
3. Swipe the timer dial near the bottom of the screen to select an exposure length.
4. Tap the **shutter** button and keep your iPhone as still as possible while the photo is taken.
5. Tap the photo thumbnail to see how the image came out.

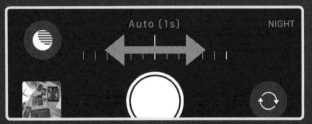

Use Night Mode to take a photo of the night sky

With an iPhone 11 Pro, you can take incredible photos of the night sky by using the Camera's maximum exposure length of 30-seconds, enabing your iPhone to capture the faint light of stars and planets.

Unlocking the 30-second exposure requires you to either use a tripod or to place the iPhone on a hard surface, because any movement will cause the image to blur. Once you've placed your iPhone on a steady surface:

1. Open the **Camera** app and set the view to either **1x** or **2x**.
2. Aim the back of the iPhone towards the night sky.
3. Either tap the **shutter** button, or if you can't see the screen press one of the **volume buttons**.
4. Leave your iPhone for 30-seconds. It's a long time to wait, especially if it's cold outdoors!
5. Open the Photos app and check out the image. For the best results, make sure there is no cloud cover or interfering light from nearby buildings.

Chapter 4

Take a portrait photo

Portrait photos are amazing. They mimic a DSLR camera by blurring the background behind a person. To do this your iPhone uses machine learning to automatically detect the face and hair of a subject, the distance between them and the background, then it blurs the background to create a beautiful 3D effect.

To use Portrait mode:

1. Open the **Camera** app and select **Portrait** mode.

2. Place the subject at least 2 feet away. If they are too close the Camera app will let you know.

3. Tap the **capture** button to take the photo.

Use Portrait Lighting to take amazing selfies

By using Portrait Lighting mode you can simulate a number of professional photographer effects and tools, such as a gold bounce card, to create even more beautiful looking photos. There are six effects to choose from:

Natural Light	**Studio Light**	**Contour Light**	**Stage Light**	**Stage Light Mono**	**High-Key Mono**
Your subject's face in sharp focus against a blurred background.	A clean look with your subject's face brightly lit.	Adds subtle shadows and highlights to the subject's face.	Your subject's face is spotlit against a deep black background.	Like Stage Light, but in black and white.	Adds a beautiful monochromatic effect.

To enable Portrait Lighting mode, open the **Camera** app and select **Portrait**. You'll see five buttons appear towards the bottom of the screen: Natural Light, Studio Light, Contour Light, Stage Light and Stage Light Mono. Select an effect by swiping through the options. Watch the screen to see the effect apply to your face in real-time. Press the **capture** button to take a photo.

You can choose another effect, even after the photo has been saved, by tapping the **Edit** button within the Photos app.

Take a photo using iPhone 11 or 11 Pro

Disable the Portrait mode effect

To disable the Portrait effect in a photo, open the image, tap **Edit**, then tap the yellow **Portrait** button at the top of the screen.

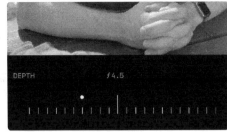

Adjust the aperture

While editing a Portrait Mode photo, tap the **f.28** button in the top corner then use the slider near the bottom of the screen to adjust the aperture (depth) of the background.

Capture outside the frame

Go to **Settings > Camera**, then toggle **Photos Capture Outside the Frame** on. Now, when you go to rotate a photo, you won't see black borders around the image.

Enable 4K video recording

To enable 4K video recording, open the **Settings** app, tap **Camera**, then select **Record Video**. On the following panel you'll be able to enable video recording at 4K.

Slow motion video

One of the most fun camera features included with iPhone is the ability to shoot video in slow motion at 240 frames per second. It's great for capturing fast-moving objects.

Film in slo-mo

While in the Camera app, swipe the text at the bottom of the screen until **SLO-MO** is centered. Next, tap the red record button to start filming your slow motion video

Edit the playback speed of a slow-mo video

To edit the slow-motion parts of a video, open the video in the **Photos** app, then tap the **Edit** button.

You'll notice a timeline at the bottom of the screen that's broken up by thin white lines. In the center the lines are spaced further apart. This is the part of the clip which plays back in slow motion.

You can lengthen or shorten this slow motion part of the clip by dragging the white handles, then preview the clip by tapping the play button.

You can also adjust the appearance of a video, crop and rotate it, or even add a filter by using the buttons along the bottom of the screen.

Chapter 4

How to use the Camera timer

To enable the timer, open the **Camera** app then tap the arrow at the top of the screen. You'll see a selection of controls appear above the shutter button. Look for the stopwatch button (it's fifth from the left), and tap it. You'll see three text options appear: **Timer Off**, **3s** and **10s**. These correspond to the timer settings, so off is the standard setting, 3s gives you three seconds to pose, and 10s gives you 10 seconds to prepare yourself. Tap whichever you need, then tap the **Shutter** button to snap a photo. You'll see a countdown appear on-screen and the camera flash will also emit a brief light for each passing second. After the countdown has ended your iPhone will quickly capture a photo and save it to your photo library.

Capture time-lapse video

Have you ever wanted to capture a sun set, the changing tides, or the movement of clouds? Using the Camera app you can do this with the time-lapse feature. It works by capturing multiple photos, instead of video, over a period of time.

To capture a time-lapse video, open the **Camera** app, then select **TIME-LAPSE**. Next, place your iPhone in a suitable location. Make sure it's steady – any movements over time will ruin the time-lapse effect. When you're ready, tap the **red record** button. Leave your iPhone for a few moments or minutes - the longer the better as you'll capture more footage - then tap the red record button again to end the time-lapse.

Capture a panoramic shot

Have you ever wanted to capture an incredibly beautiful vista? By using the PANO mode you can do just this by taking a super-wide, 180-degree photo.

PANO mode works by taking one very wide continuous photo. As you rotate on the spot, the camera captures the image as it appears on the right side of the lens. If there's any movement in front of you (such as people walking by), then you might see a few visual errors, but for vistas and still scenes the PANO mode works wonders.

1. Open the **Camera** app and select **PANO** mode.

2. You'll see a thumbnail in the center of the screen with a white arrow pointing right.

3. Tap the **Camera** button at the bottom of the screen to start capturing a panoramic shot.

4. Slowly pan your device to the right. Keep a steady hand — if you wobble too much black bars will appear at the top and bottom of the photo.

5. Tap the **thumbnail** in the bottom corner to check out your panoramic image.

Chapter 4

Camera filters

Filters enable you to instantly alter the appearance of a photo. There are nine to choose from: Vivid, Vivid Warm, Vivid Cool, Dramatic, Dramatic Warm, Dramatic Cool, Mono, Silvertone, and Noir.

Access the filters

To add a filter, open the **Camera** app then tap the **arrow** at the top of the screen. A selection of controls will appear above the shutter button. Tap the filter button on the far right.

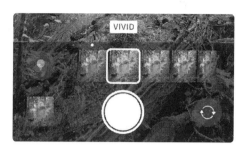

Choose a filter

You'll instantly see all eight filters previewed on the screen. Tap on one and the filter will be applied to any photos you take.

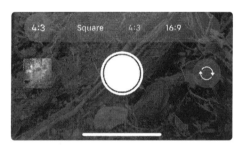

Adjust the aspect ratio

By default, photos are captured in a 4:3 ratio. To swap to a cinematic 16:9 or square 1:1, tap the **arrow** in the top-center of the screen, then tap the **4:3** button above the shutter. You'll then see shortcut buttons for swapping to another aspect ratio.

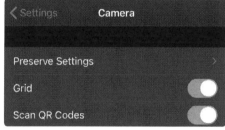

Enable the camera grid

Taking level photos can be tricky when only using the preview window, so to help line up horizons, try enabling the camera grid. To do this, go to **Settings > Camera**, then toggle the **Grid** button on.

Next, go back to the Camera app and you'll see a 3x3 grid above the preview window.

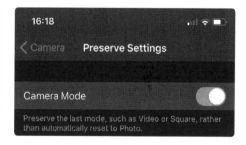

Preserve Camera Settings

Every time you close the Camera app, then re-open it, it defaults back to the Camera mode; no matter what you were doing before. If you want to reuse a specific mode, such as the video camera, swiping back to it over and over again can be a real pain. Thankfully, there's an easy way to preserve the camera mode you were using last. Just go to **Settings > Camera > Preserve Settings** and toggle **Camera Mode** on.

Camera and Photos

View and edit your Photos

Learn how to view, organize, and edit your photos...

The Photos app is a portal to your memories. Stored within its colorful icon are hundreds, if not thousands of treasured photos and videos. Photos of yapping dogs, family members, stunning landscapes, unflattering selfies, and treasured holidays. This is one of those apps that you're going to be opening on a day-to-day basis, so keep it somewhere prominent on the Home screen where you can quickly tap it.

Open the app, and you'll discover a clean, tidy interface that appears to be basic and easy to use. In many ways it is, but dig a little deeper, and you'll find one of the most productive and in-depth apps available on iPhone. With just one fingertip it's possible to edit photos, create albums, move and delete images, view memories, and much more.

To find the Photos app, look for the colorful flower icon:

The basics of using the Photos app

1. Tap on the small plus/minus button to zoom in and out. You can also pinch to zoom into your photos.

2. Tap on a day, month or year to zoom into that date, or alternatively keep tapping inwards.

3. Tap the **Photos** button to come back to this view, where you can see an overview of all your snaps.

4. Tap on **For You** to see a memory of a day trip, a birthday, a family gathering, or even a "Best of 2019" album.

5. Tap **Albums** to view categories of photos, videos, people, slow-mo videos, and more.

6. Select **Search** to look for nearly anything in a photo, including both people and objects.

All Photos

When viewing All Photos, you'll see a nearly endless grid of photos scrolling upwards and off the screen. You can scroll through them and tap on an image to see it bigger, or you can pinch to zoom in or out to see your photos spread over a wider range of time.

Days

Tap on the Days button and you'll see a beautiful grid of images representing a single day. The Photos app intelligently organizes your images, hiding duplicates while selecting a highlighted image or video.

Months

The Months view organizes the most meaningful events into groups, then displays them as individual cards in a scrollable panel. The app tries to intelligently select the best photo or video to remind you of what the event was about. Think of it as a greatest hit library of your memories.

Years

Years gives you a high-level overview of your photo library, but what makes this view really special is it's dynamic and based on context. So open the Years view on your birthday and you'll see photos from your birthday celebrations going back as far as your photo library extends.

ew and edit your Photos

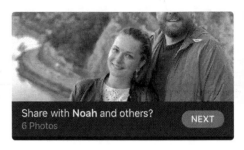

Photos

Tap on the **Photos** button at the bottom of the screen and you'll see every photo ever taken using your iPhone. You can zoom out to see more images by tapping the blue arrow in the top-left corner. Tap it again and it'll zoom even further out...

The Photos app instantly reads the location and time data within each photo and uses them to sort the images. So if you're on holiday in San Francisco and take 10 photos by the Golden Gate Bridge, these will appear as a moment in the Photos app, titled "*Bay Bridge, San Francisco CA*".

For You

Next to the Photos button at the bottom of the screen is **For You**. This is one of the most powerful features of the Photos app. It works by organizing your images into events and albums, then presents these events in chronological order for you to enjoy.

Every day a new set of moments, people, and categories will appear. Tap on one and you'll see more details about the moment, including the location and date.

Share an event

Whenever the For You section displays a new moment, it will offer the ability to share the corresponding photos with whoever is included in the moment, so if you go hiking with a buddy, the Photos app will let you share all the images with them in just a few steps. Here's how:

1. Select one of the moments in the **Sharing Suggestions** field.
2. If someone you know appears in the photos, tap **Next**.
3. On the following panel, tap **Share in Messages**.
4. You can also add additional people from your contacts list by tapping **+ Add People**.

Watch a video of an event

Whenever the Photos app suggests a moment, it will also offer the ability to watch it back as a video. To do this:

1. Open the **Photos** app, tap **For You**, then choose a moment which appears.
2. Tap the small blue **options** button in the top-right corner.
3. Select **Play Movie** from the pop-up field.

Edit a memory video

1. Begin playing the video, then pause it.
2. Notice the **options** above the scrub bar. They enable you to choose a theme and adjust the overall length of the video.
3. Tap on a theme (such as **Gentle** or **Happy**), then press **play** to see the changes made.
4. Similarly, tap on a new duration then press **play** to see the changes.
5. To save the video, tap the **Share** button in the bottom left corner then choose **Save Video**.

Chapter 4

Search through your photos

The Photos app is incredibly intelligent. Using complex visual algorithms it can recognize objects, faces and places, then automatically organize groups of images into albums for you to enjoy. This clever form of visual recognition has another benefit: intelligent searching. You can access this search feature at any time by tapping the **Search** button at the bottom of the screen.

Search for "*California*" and you'll see all your photos of California. Search for "*Trees*" and you'll see (you guessed it) images of trees. You can be even more specific. So search for "*Trees in California*" and the Photos app will automatically show photos of trees within California. You can try other queries such as "*Tom eating pizza*", or "*Sarah riding a horse*" and the app will instantly present you with the correct results.

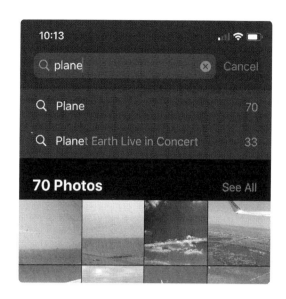

People and Places

After scanning every photo in your library to look for photos of locations and faces, the Photos app collates them into the **People and Places** section of the Photos app.

Find People and Places

To see these images just open the Photos app and go to **Albums > People & Places**.

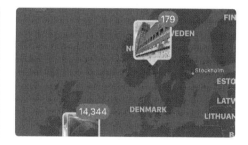

Check out the places view

Tap on the **Places** thumbnail, and you'll see a map view with all of your photos placed in the correct location.

Watch a video of someone

To watch a video of someone in the People album, select them then tap the **play** button near the top of the screen.

Add a name to a person

To add a name to someone in the People album, tap the **+ Add Name** field at the top of the screen.

Add someone to Favorites

If you like to regularly see the photos of a family member or friend, tap the small **heart** icon in the bottom corner of their thumbnail image.

125

...w and edit your Photos

How to share a photo or video

Open an image, then tap the **Share** icon in the bottom-left corner of the screen – it looks like a blue box with an arrow pointing upwards.

Select multiple images

To select multiple photos at once, make sure you're viewing a collection of images then tap the blue **Select** button in the top-right corner of the screen.

How to delete a photo

While viewing an image tap the blue **Trash** icon in the bottom- right corner of the screen.

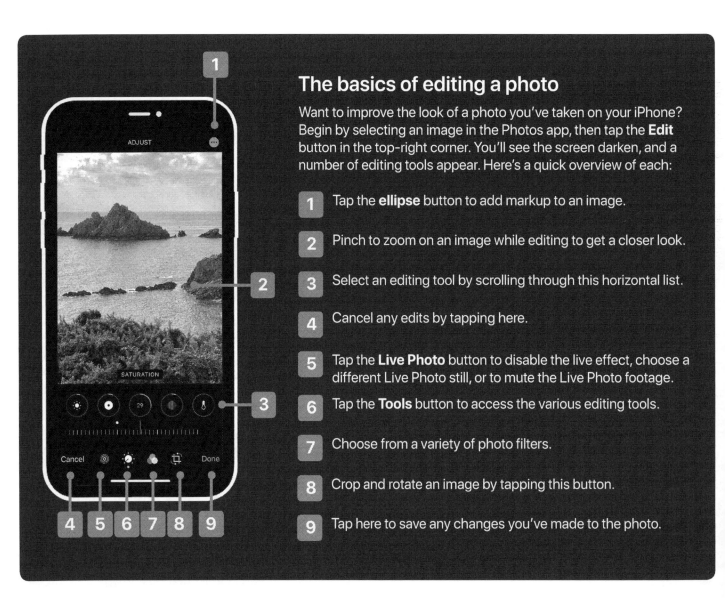

The basics of editing a photo

Want to improve the look of a photo you've taken on your iPhone? Begin by selecting an image in the Photos app, then tap the **Edit** button in the top-right corner. You'll see the screen darken, and a number of editing tools appear. Here's a quick overview of each:

1. Tap the **ellipse** button to add markup to an image.
2. Pinch to zoom on an image while editing to get a closer look.
3. Select an editing tool by scrolling through this horizontal list.
4. Cancel any edits by tapping here.
5. Tap the **Live Photo** button to disable the live effect, choose a different Live Photo still, or to mute the Live Photo footage.
6. Tap the **Tools** button to access the various editing tools.
7. Choose from a variety of photo filters.
8. Crop and rotate an image by tapping this button.
9. Tap here to save any changes you've made to the photo.

Chapter 4

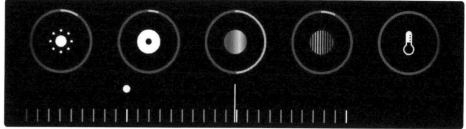

Adjustment tools

The second icon at the bottom of the screen enables you to adjust the appearance of an image. When you tap this button, the auto-correct tool is initially selected. Tap this tool to automatically improve the look of an image.

Fine tune an image

By dragging the tools to the left, you can horizontally scroll through them. You'll see tools for adjusting a photos exposure, brilliance, highlights, shadows, contrast, brightness, black point, saturation, color, warmth, tint, sharpness, noise and vignette. Select a tool then use the horizontal slider below to make fine adjustments. By experimenting with each tool, you'll discover your own favorite settings and adjustments.

Disable an adjustment tool

To disable and reset an adjustment tool, simply tap on its button. You'll see the button go grey and any adjustments will reset.

Add a vignette

Scroll all the way to the left and you'll find the Vignette tool. Drag the slider to the left to add a white vignette effect, and to the right to add a dark vignette.

Compare changes to a photo

If you'd like to compare your changes with the original photo at any time, tap and hold your finger on the thumbnail image above the editing controls.

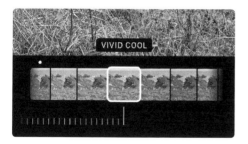

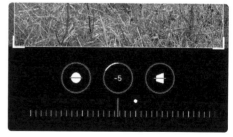

Add a filter

The middle icon at the bottom of the screen enables you to add a photo filter to your image. You'll find eight to choose from, each with its own unique appearance.

Crop an image

Tap the **Crop** icon, then either drag the edges of the image to crop it, or tap the small **ratio** button in the top-right corner to choose from a range of image ratio sizes.

Rotate or tilt a photo

While cropping a photo you can also rotate or tilt it. To rotate an image, just drag the horizontal slider below the image. To tilt an image, tap one of the two tilt buttons then drag the same horizontal slider.

127

Bring a flat image to life

Photos taken using iPhone usually look amazing, but on occasion can look a little flat or overblown due to the small lens and sensor. Thankfully, the Photos app makes it easy to turn flat images into colorful, expressive shots. Here's how it's done:

1 Start by editing a photo
Select an image using the Photos app, then tap the **Edit** button in the top-right corner.

2 Adjust the brilliance
Scroll through the editing tools until **Brilliance** is selected. Now, pull the slider to the right using your finger and watch as colors and depth are revealed.

3 Adjust the highlights
Scroll through the editing tools again and choose **Highlights**, then drag the slider to the left and watch how as even more colors appear.

4 Edit the Shadows
Drag the slider along by one tool to select **Shadows**, then drag the slider to the right by a small amount. You'll see darker areas of the image become brighter and more colorful.

5 Color Adjustments
Next, select the **Colors** tool, then drag the slider left using your finger to subtlety boost the colors of the photo.

6 Further adjustments
Other tools you can experiment with include contrast, warmth and tint. Feel free to experiment, with time you'll discover which tools work best with various scenarios and lighting conditions, and soon you'll be able to improve a photo in just a few seconds.

Before and after making adjustments to an image.

Chapter 4

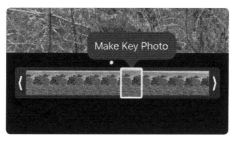

Edit Live Photos

Live Photos are amazing. They're like the magical moving photos you might have seen in the Harry Potter movies, but they work with your photos. It's also possible to trim the video snippets before or after the photo, select a new keyframe, disable the audio or even change the visual effect animation of the Live photo. Read on to find out how...

Select a new key frame

If you've taken an action shot and noticed that the exact moment you wanted to capture is in the moving segment of the Live Photo, then you can easily edit the photo and select the exact frame as your key photo. To do this open the photo, tap the **Edit** button, tap the **Live Photo** button, then use the timeline scrubber to choose the new key frame. Once you've found it, tap **Make Key Photo**.

Trim a Live Photo

Sometimes you might want to trim a part of the Live Photo effect. For example, maybe you suddenly moved the camera at the very last second. Whatever the reason, it's easy to trim the beginning or end.

To get started, select the photo, tap the **Edit** button, then tap the **Live Photo** button. Next, use the handles on either side of the timeline scrubber to fine-tune the start or endpoints.

Change the animation effect of your Live Photo

The photos app includes some amazing Live Photo effects that can be applied to your image. To apply one, simply open the Live Photo you wish to edit then slide the screen upwards with your finger. You'll see the Effects panel appear beneath. Just tap on the effect of choice to preview and use it.

Live
The standard Live Photo effect. To watch it playback, just tap and hold on the photo.

Loop
This effect turns your Live Photo into a never-ending video loop. If you've ever seen GIF images on the web you'll know how this looks. It works best when the camera is perfectly still, or when there is little movement in the Live Photo.

Bounce
Bounce works in a similar way to the Loop effect, except instead of starting the Live Photo again, it plays in reverse once it reaches the end of the clip.

Long Exposure
This effect works by combining all the frames of your Live Photo into one image. For the best effect, hold your iPhone while taking a photo. Water looks ethereal and misty when viewed through the Long Exposure effect, while moving traffic blurs and streaks across the image.

View and edit your Photos

Turn off the Live Photo sound

If you don't want to hear the background noise of a Live Photo then select the image, tap the **Edit** button, select the **Live Photo** tool, then tap the yellow **sound** button in the upper-left corner to mute (or unmute) the audio.

Hide photos

If you'd like to hide a photo from the Photos, Memories and Shared albums, open the photo, tap the **Share** button, scroll down then tap **Hide**. Note that the photo will be copied to a new Hidden album where you can un-hide it if necessary.

Trim and edit videos

Open a video, tap the **Edit** button and you'll find the same image editing tools, which means you can adjust the light and color of a video, rotate it and even add filters.

You can also trim the beginning and end of a video to adjust its timing and length. To do this tap **Edit** then make a note of the timeline which appears just above the editing tools. By dragging the handles on each side of the timeline you can adjust the start and end points of the video.

Create an album

If you'd like to organize your photos and videos into albums then tap the **Albums** button at the bottom of the screen. If you've taken or synced any photos then you'll likely see a number of albums already present, including Videos, Burst Mode photos and Slo-mos.

To add an additional album, just tap the blue **plus** icon at the top of the screen. A pop-up window will appear asking for an album title. Enter one using the on-screen keyboard, then tap the **Save** button.

You'll then see a window appear which contains all the available photos on your device. Tap on as many images as you'd like, then tap the **Done** button at the top of the screen. These images will now be added to your new album.

Chapter 4

Rename an album

While viewing the main Albums screen tap the **Edit** button. Existing albums such as Recently Added and Recently Deleted can't be re-named, but any albums added by yourself can. Tap on the title of the album and the keyboard will slide up the screen. Update or change the album name, then tap the **Done** button to confirm the changes.

Move an image from one album to another

To move an image from one album to another, select an image then tap the **Share** button. In the pop-up panel, choose **Add to Album**, then select the album you wish to copy the image too.

Delete an album

It's easy to delete albums from your iPhone. From the Albums screen, tap the **Edit** button in the top-right corner. Small red buttons will appear alongside any albums you've created. Tap any of these and the album will be deleted from your iPhone.

Create a shared album

By using shared albums, it's possible to share a selection of images with your friends and family. They can leave comments, like photos, and save them to their device. Here's how it works:

1. Tap the **Albums** button at the bottom of the screen.

2. Tap the **plus** icon in the top-left corner, then choose **New Shared Album**.

3. In the pop-up window, give the album a name (such as "*Holiday*"), then tap the **Next** button.

4. On the following panel select contacts to share the album with. You can tap their name to enter a contact, or tap the **plus** icon to select people from your contacts book.

5. Once you've added a bunch of friends or family, tap the **Create** button. The blank album will appear on-screen, to add photos and videos just tap the blue text that reads **Add Photos or Videos**.

Apps, Music, and Videos

With the App Store, the iPhone becomes one of the most powerful and versatile devices in the world, with access to a nearly limitless amount of content and features.

Similarly, if you're an Apple Music subscriber, then you have the world's music at your fingertips, whenever and wherever you are. With Apple Music you can stream the latest tracks, download entire albums to your iPhone, and even watch exclusive TV shows; and even if you're not a subscriber, then it's still possible to purchase and download music from the iTunes Store.

Contents:

Install and manage apps	134
Listen to Music	136
Watch TV & Movies	140

Apps, Music, and Video

Install and manage apps

Explore the App Store and manage third-party apps...

The iPhone is already a versatile device, with an amazing web browser, email client, great camera and more. But with a nearly endless supply of apps available within the App Store, you can do truly magical things with iPhone. You can interact with books in new ways, edit high-definition video and photos, order takeaway food, and much more.

To find the App Store, just look for the blue icon with a white A over the top:

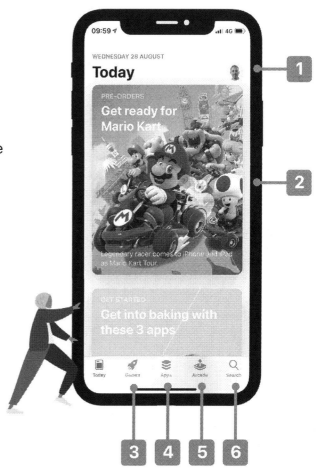

The basics of using the App Store

1. Tap on your profile photo to edit your Apple ID, see recent purchases, or redeem gift cards.

2. From the Today view, tap on a card to find out more about the best apps of the day.

3. Tap **Games** to browse the latest free and paid for games.

4. Tap **Apps** to browse app categories, see the latest charts, plus a curated list of apps by Apple.

5. Tap **Arcade** to subscribe to Apple Arcade, where you'll find 100s of exclusive titles to play.

6. Use **Search** to find an app you're looking for, or see the latest trends.

Chapter 5

How to install an app

To install an app, just tap the **GET** button if it's a free app, or the **price** button if it's a paid app. Enter your Apple ID password and the app will be added to the Home screen.

In-app purchases

Wondering why that amazing-looking app is free? Chances are it has in-app purchases. If so, the text "In-App Purchases" will be displayed below the Get or price button.

Get support for an app

To find support for an app, locate it within the App Store, scroll down to the Reviews section, then tap the **App Support** button.

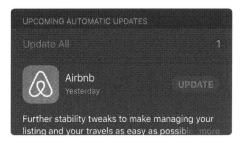

Check for app updates

To see if any app updates are available, open the App Store, tap on your **profile image** in the top-right corner, then scroll down to the UPCOMING AUTOMATIC UPDATES area.

Subscribe to Apple Arcade

If you regularly play games on your iPhone, then Apple Arcade might be just up your alley. With one monthly subscription, you can play more than 100 games for free, download and play offline, and sync your saves across all of your devices. To find Apple Arcade open the **App Store**, tap on **Arcade** at the bottom of the screen, then follow the on-screen instructions to subscribe.

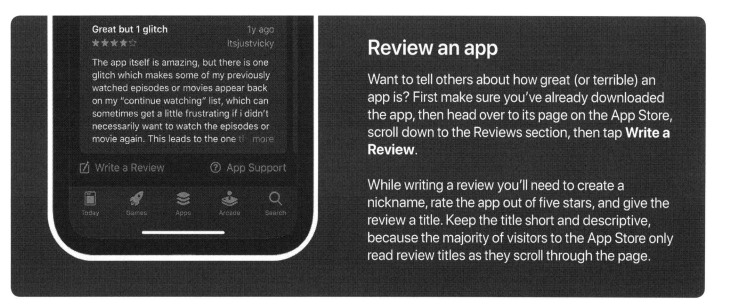

Review an app

Want to tell others about how great (or terrible) an app is? First make sure you've already downloaded the app, then head over to its page on the App Store, scroll down to the Reviews section, then tap **Write a Review**.

While writing a review you'll need to create a nickname, rate the app out of five stars, and give the review a title. Keep the title short and descriptive, because the majority of visitors to the App Store only read review titles as they scroll through the page.

135

Apps, Music, and Video

Listen to Music

Listen to your favorite tracks and albums on Apple Music...

The Music app has always been the best way to listen to music on iPhone. It has a beautiful interface, access to millions of tracks via Apple Music, exclusive TV shows, curated playlists, videos, top charts, and Beats 1 Radio.

There's a limitless source of music available in Apple Music, but it comes at a price: to access the full service you'll need to pay a monthly subscription. It's priced slightly differently for each country but roughly works out about the same as a large takeaway pizza. For anyone who listens to the latest charts, streams music on a daily basis or has a wide variety of music tastes, it's definitely worth the asking price. For everyone else, Apple Music still offers Beats 1 Radio, the ability to follow artists and preview music.

To find the Music app on your iPhone, just look for this icon:

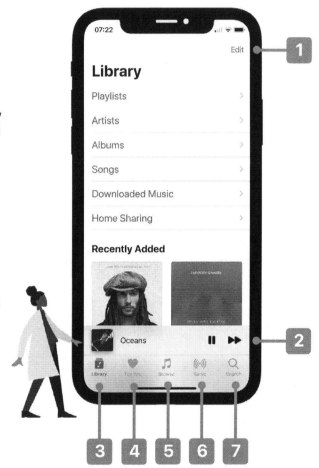

The basics of using Music

1. Tap **Edit** to add or remove common shortcuts to your playlists, artists, albums, and more.

2. While a song is playing, tap on this panel to access playback controls.

3. Tap **Library** to access all the music, playlists, and albums saved on your iPhone.

4. Tap **For You** to see playlists created by Apple which suit your tastes, your listening history, what friends are listening too, and new releases.

5. Tap **Browse** and you'll find the latest tracks, top charts, music videos, and TV shows exclusive to Apple Music.

6. Tap **Radio** to discover a wide range of radio stations for every taste.

7. To **Search** to find songs, albums, artists, or lyrics. Either saved on your iPhone or on Apple Music.

Chapter 5

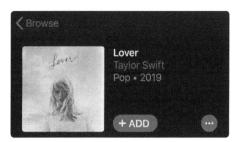

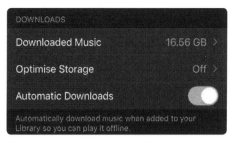

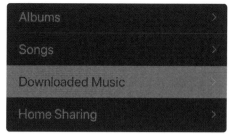

Add music to your Library

If there's a track or album that you'd like to save to your Library, tap the **+Add** button at the top of the screen.

Automatically download music

To automatically download music to your iPhone whenever you add a new album or track, open the **Settings** app, tap **Music** then toggle **Automatic Downloads** on.

Browse your offline music

If you don't have a signal and need to play music that's saved to your iPhone, tap on **Library** then choose **Downloaded Music**.

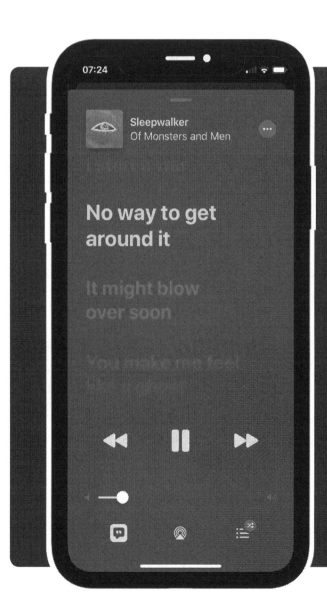

View music lyrics in realtime

Have you ever struggled to understand the lyrics of a song as it plays in the background? With iOS 13 you can now get fullscreen lyrics for all your favorite songs, and they update in realtime so you can follow along with the song. Think of it as your own karaoke machine. Here's how it works:

When listening to a song, tap on the small lyrics button in the bottom-left corner of the screen. It looks like a small speech bubble. You'll then see a fullscreen lyrics view take over. If you don't see the **lyrics** button, just make sure you're looking at the music playback window. You can get to it at any moment by opening the Music app then tapping on the small album artwork thumbnail at the bottom of the screen.

Apps, Music, and Video

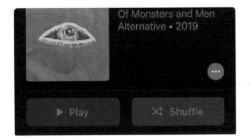

Shuffle music

If you're bored of an album track order, tap **Shuffle** and you'll never know what song is coming up next.

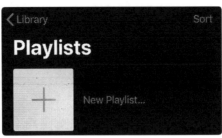

Create a Playlist

To create a new playlist of your own, tap **Library**, select **Playlists**, then choose **New Playlist**.

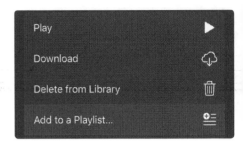

Add music to an existing playlist

If you'd like to add a track to an existing playlist, tap and hold on the track then choose **Add to a Playlist...** in the Share sheet. This also works with albums too.

Delete a track or album

Fed up with a song or album? Just tap and hold on the track name or album artwork, then tap **Delete from Library** in the Share sheet.

Like music to improve your recommendations list

Whenever you hear a great track or album, tap the **options** button in the corner of the screen (it looks like three dots) then tap the **Love** button. This tells Apple Music what genre of music you like. Keep doing this and over time the For You playlists and recommendations will get more and more accurate to your tastes in music.

Turn off Apple Music

If you'd like to turn off Apple Music and only see music purchased from the iTunes Store or synced to your device, go to **Settings > Music**, then un-toggle **Show Apple Music**.

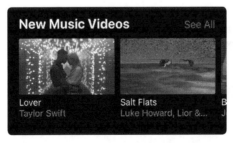

Check out the latest music videos

To browse the latest music videos, open the Music app, tap **Browse**, scroll down then tap **Music Videos**. Tap on a video to watch it, then hold your iPhone horizontally to see it full screen.

See the top charts

What to see what's number one in the charts? Open the **Music** app, tap **Browse**, then tap **Top Charts**.

Chapter 5

Share your music

When you open the Music app for the first time, you'll be asked if you would like to share your music with friends and family. You can tap **Get Started** to set this feature up straight away, or if you'd like to do it later just tap the **For You** button, tap your **user icon** in the top-right corner, then tap the **Edit** button below your name. Here's how it works:

1. Start by choosing a profile photo and user name.

2. Tap **Next**, then decide if anyone can follow you, or just those you approve.

3. Choose if you would like to show your custom playlists within your profile or in search on Apple Music.

4. Invite your friends to follow you on Apple Music. You can also connect to Facebook to add friends not in your contact book.

5. Tap **Next** and choose whether you would like to receive notifications when your friends start following you, when they add new playlists, or when there's a new release or mix by one of your favorite artists.

6. Tap **Done** and you're ready to go.

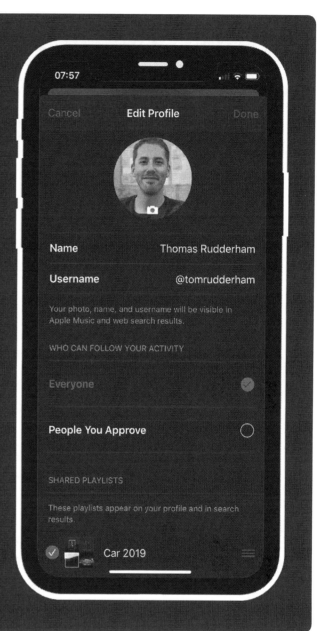

139

Apps, Music, and Video

Watch TV & Movies

Never miss an episode of your favorite show with this helpful app...

With so many sources of video content these days, it has become difficult to keep track of the latest episodes of your favorite TV shows. Thankfully, the TV app for iPhone makes it a little bit easier, by collating many of the latest releases into one app. It also houses any TV shows or movies which you've purchased on iTunes, and remembers where you last left off.

To find the TV app on your iPhone, just search for it using Spotlight, or look for this icon:

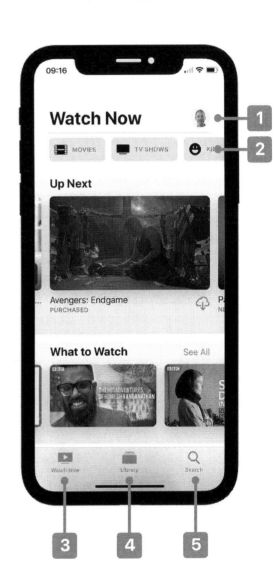

The basics of using TV

1 Tap on your profile photo to manage subscriptions, redeem a Gift Card, or sign out.

2 Quickly jump between movies, TV, or kids shows with these helpful shortcuts.

3 If you're looking for inspiration, tap **Watch Now** to find suggested TV shows and movies.

4 You'll find all of your purchases in the **Library** section of the app, split into TV Shows and Movies.

4 It's pretty obvious, but by tapping **Search** you can look for movies, TV shows, or cast and crew.

Chapter 5

Watch HDR movies on your iPhone

If you've purchased any movies with support for HDR playback, tap on **Library,** then scroll down to see a list of HDR-compatible films.

Find the top rentals

From the **Watch Now** area, scroll down until you find the More to Explore panel. Scroll to the left and you'll find a shortcut to the most popular movie rentals.

See what's available on Apple TV+

Apple TV+ promises to be a serious competitor to Netflix and Amazon Prime. You can see what's available and coming soon by tapping **Watch Now** then scrolling down.

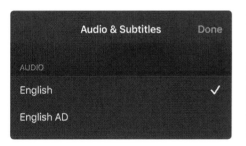

Toggle audio sources or subtitles

While watching a video, tap the **speech** icon next to the playback timer to toggle different audio sources or subtitles.

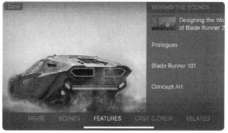

Access movie special features

To access special features or scene shortcuts, watch a movie in landscape mode. You'll see buttons for special features appear along the bottom of the screen.

Watch on your Apple TV

If you want to watch a video on your TV, tap the **Apple TV** icon in the bottom-right corner while a video is playing, then choose your Apple TV.

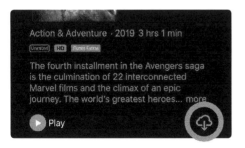

Download a film to your iPhone

If you want to save a purchased film to your iPhone, tap on its **artwork,** then tap the **iCloud** button.

Find out more about cast or crew

Search for an actor, producer, director, or other member of crew, and you can see what films they've been in, created, or made a guest appearance.

141

Maps, News, and Utilities

It doesn't seem so long ago that paper maps were the norm. Physical, cumbersome things which people carried around in their cars or backpacks. Now, with the iPhone at your fingertips, it's possible to navigate the globe and never get lost.

The iPhone also makes for a powerful utility tool too. It has a helpful notes app, can check the latest news, and much more...

Contents:

Use Maps to navigate the world	144
Get the latest news	148
Monitor the stock market	150
Create Reminders	152
Create your own Siri Shortcuts	154
Create, edit, and share Notes	156
Manage your Files	160

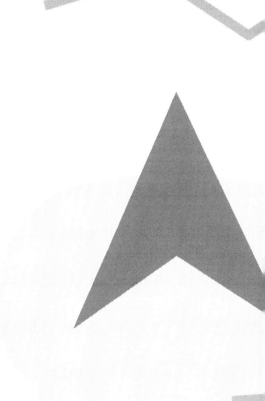

Maps, News, and Utilities

Use Maps to navigate the world

Discover new places, get route guidance, and more...

With a map of the entire globe in your pocket, it's no longer possible to get lost in a busy city or strange new land. That's exactly what the Maps app gives you, alongside directions, real-time traffic information, transit timetables, 3D views of major cities and more. All of this for free and accessible at any time.

To find the Map app, just unlock your iPhone then tap on this icon:

The basics of using Maps

1 This blue dot represents your current location in the world.

3 This is the main map view. You can pan and zoom using your fingers.

2 Tap the **Info** button to change the view, toggle traffic, or mark your location.

4 Tap on the **search field** to search for a place, address, or landmark.

5 Notice the information bar at the bottom of the screen. This automatically displays your recent activity, so you might see how long it will take to get home, where your car is parked, or where an event in your calendar is happening. You'll also find any collections of places you've saved alongside recently viewed locations.

144

Chapter 6

See a 3D map

Using the Maps app it's possible to navigate the world's most famous cities in beautiful 3D graphics. To view the 3D map, ensure you're in satellite mode (see step above) then zoom in on the map. When you're close to the ground, you'll notice a **3D** button appear in the upper-right corner. Tap it and the Maps view will tilt, then load a 3D landscape with detailed 3D buildings. To rotate the image, simply place two fingers on the screen then rotate them. To tilt the camera, simultaneously move two fingers up or down the screen. Moving them left or right will pan the camera.

Take a Look Around in first-person

Chances are you've seen Google's Street View. It's a great piece of technology that lets you explore the world at street level using full 360-degree imagery. Apple's Look Around mode is similar, but it's more polished, realistic, and includes tags for exploring businesses and interesting locations.

To use the Look Around mode, zoom the map until you see a binocular icon appear in the top-right corner. At the time of writing, it will only appear in major cities within the United States. Once you see it, tap the icon, and the map view will zoom down to street level.

To pan the view, just push it with your finger. To move in any direction, double-tap where you want to go. You can also tap on a tag to see more information about the place or business.

One last tip: tap the **minimize** icon in the top-left corner to shrink the Look Around view and place it above the 2D map. You can now move the Look Around view by panning the map with your finger.

Maps, News, and Utilities: Use Maps to navigate the world

Enjoy a flyover tour

Want to explore a city like never before? Simply search for the city's name then tap the **Flyover** button in the information panel at the bottom of the screen.

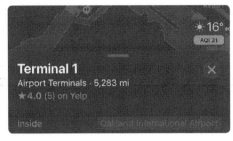

Search indoor maps

With the Maps app you can find your way around airports and shopping centers using the indoor maps feature, which displays the locations of stores, toilets, and more.

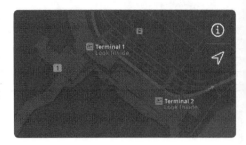

"Look Inside"

Most international airports and major shopping centers are fuly mapped. Just look for a "look inside" badge that appears beneath the name of the location.

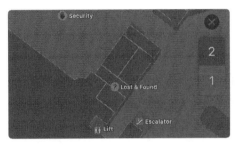

Navigate floors

If there are multiple floors to the building, you can navigate through them by tapping the number button on the right-side of the screen, just beneath the info buttons.

See Transit information

If you're exploring a location using public transport then it's a good idea to view the local area using the Transit view in Maps. This lets you see nearby train stations, tube lines, bus stations, taxi pick-up points and more. To enable this view simply tap the **Info** icon in the top-right corner of the screen then choose **Transport**.

Drop a pin to find out more

To see detailed information about a specific point, simply tap and hold your finger on the screen and a pin will be dropped underneath it.

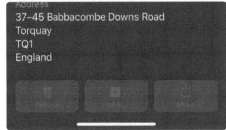

Share a location

Want to send an address to friends and family? Just search for the location then tap the **Share** icon in the information panel at the bottom of the screen.

Search Maps using Siri

If you'd rather search for a place or person using Siri, hold down the **Power** button until Siri appears, then say something like *"where is the nearest hotel?"*

Chapter 6

Turn-by-turn navigation

Satellite navigation and GPS technology have made driving to unfamiliar locations so much easier; and with an iPhone, you can take advantage of this same technology to explore and navigate the world. It's wonderfully easy to use. Once set up, Maps will display the route in 3D, with road signs, written directions, and spoken directions. And if the traffic conditions change, Maps will offer an alternative route for you to take.

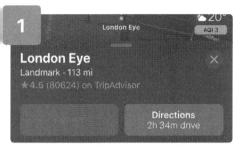

To get started, open Maps then tap the **Search** field in the information panel. Next, enter the destination you wish the navigate too. This can be an address, zip code, or you can tap and hold on the map to drop a pin.

Once you've searched for an address tap the blue **Directions** button to enable turn-by-turn instructions. Maps will automatically find the optimal route to the destination. It will also offer alternative routes, if any are available, which appear as opaque blue lines on the map. You can tap on these alternative routes to choose them.

Once you've found a suitable route tap the green **GO** button to begin following turn-by-turn directions.

Maps will automatically speak directions out-loud when you approach turns, lane changes, and exits - just as you'd expect if using a dedicated Sat-Nav device. You can even press the **Power** button to turn off your iPhone display and it will light up whenever a change in direction is needed.

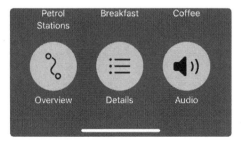

Mute or adjust voice commands

To turn off the Siri voice commands pull the information panel upwards from the bottom of the screen, tap the **Audio** button then select the relevant option.

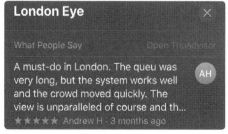

Check out location reviews

If you're planning a trip to somewhere popular, search for it then pull the information panel upwards. Further down the panel you'll find a list of visitor reviews.

Report an issue with the map

To report an error or missing place, tap the **Info** button in the top-right corner of the screen then tap **Report an Issue**.

Maps, News, and Utilities

Get the latest news

View the latest headlines and featured articles...

With the News app on iPhone, you'll find all the latest news stories and featured articles in one place. That's because the News app automatically collects all the stories and topics you're interested in and presents them together. It also combines the rich design language typically found in traditional print, along with the interactivity of the web, to create an immersive experience where the story comes to life like never before.

To find the News app on your iPhone, search for it using Spotlight, or look for this icon:

Get started

Open the News app for the first time and you'll be greeted by the Get Started screen. From here you can add news sources, and sign up for an email newsletter than sends you the best stories each day.

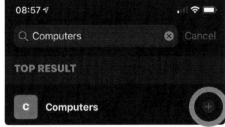

Add a news source

Once the app is set up and running it's just as easy to add and customize your news sources. Tap the **Following** button at the bottom of the screen, enter a channel or topic name then tap the plus icon.

Remove news sources

To remove news sources tap the **Following** button, tap **Edit** at the top of the screen then tap the delete icon that appears over each channel or topic.

Chapter 6

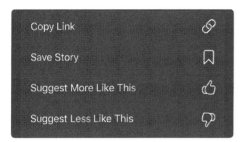

Tell News what you like

If you really like a story or topic, tap the **share** icon at the top of the screen, scroll down then tap **Suggest More Like This.** Similarly, you can also tap **Suggest Less Like This** to hide similar stories.

Save a story for later

Tap the **share** icon at the top of the screen, then tap **Save Story**. You can later find this story, along with any others you have saved, by tapping **Following**, then **Saved Stories**.

Change the text size

If you're struggling to read the text within an article, tap the **AA** button in the top-right corner, then choose a larger font size.

See your reading history

If you read a story recently and want to re-read or reference it, tap the **Following** button at the bottom of the screen, scroll down then tap the **History** button.

Tap and hold for extra options

Try tapping and holding on a story, channel or topic. You'll see a pop-up window appear with options for copying a link, following channels, opening a story in Safari and more.

Check out Apple News+

With Apple News+ you can access more than 300 periodicals for $9.99 per month after a month-long trial. To find it just tap on the News+ button at the bottom of the screen.

149

Maps, News, and Utilities

Monitor the stock market

Monitor the latest stocks and news, straight from your iPhone…

Whether you're keeping an eye on the latest stocks, betting against them, or monitoring your portfolio, the Stocks app is a helpful way to track stocks and news.

The Stocks app comes pre-installed on every iPhone. You can find it by looking for this icon:

Open the Stocks app, and the first thing you see is an overview of the leading 5 stocks, with the latest news stories at the bottom of the screen.

To add a new stock, tap on the **Search** field near the top of the screen, and search for either the company name or its stock name. Once you've found it, tap the green **plus** button to add it.

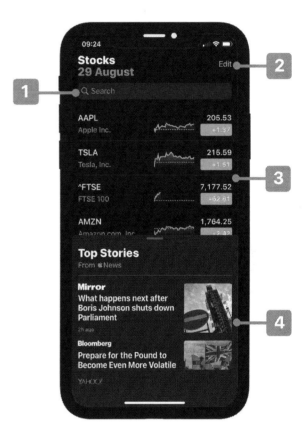

The basics of using Stocks

1 If you need to check a stock, use this search bar to find it.

2 Tap the **Edit** button in the bottom-right corner to organize your stock view.

3 Here you'll find live updates of all your stocks. Tap on one to see more information.

4 The News panel at the bottom of the screen offers an overview of the latest stock news. Tap it to see more news, or tap on an article to read it straight away.

Chapter 6

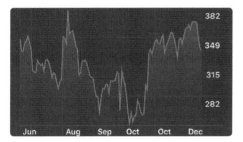

See an individual stock

Tap on an individual stock and you'll see a graph of its latest performance. If it's colored green, then the stock is doing well. If it's red, then (you guessed it) it's not performing well.

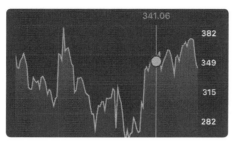

See an exact stock figure

Place your finger over a point on the share graph, and you'll see the exact figure of the stock during that day and time.

See news stories related to stocks

Scroll down and you'll see news for that particular stock, tap on one and you can read the full story.

Return to the main stock window

To go back to the main Stocks window, pull the individual stock view down from the top of the screen.

Rearrange your stocks

To rearrange the Stocks on the home panel of the app, tap the small **menu** button in the bottom-right corner of the screen, then drag the stocks up or down using the sort buttons.

Delete a stock

From the options panel you can also delete stocks by tapping the red **delete** buttons.

Maps, News, and Utilities

Create Reminders

Set yourself reminders so you'll never forget a thing...

The iPhone already includes a notes app that can be used to jot down ideas and thoughts, but Reminders makes it easy to create to-do lists, set deadlines, and organize your life. It can also remind you with alerts at pre-determined times.

That's not all the app does, of course. It can group reminders into categories and even automatically sync reminders across all your devices via iCloud. To find the Reminders app, use Spotlight, or look for this icon:

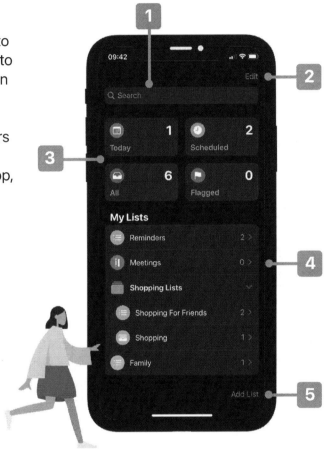

The basics of using Reminders

1 To search for reminders or lists, pull the whole screen down, then tap on the search field.

3 These helpful shortcuts enable you to jump straight to scheduled reminders or flagged items.

5 To create a new list or reminder, just tap this button in the bottom-right corner.

2 Tap **Edit** to re-arrange or delete multiple lists and reminders.

4 You can re-arrange your lists by tapping, holding, then dragging. You can also swipe them towards the left to access further options.

Chapter 6

Create a new Reminder

From the home screen of the Reminders app, tap the **Reminders** option under My Lists, then tap **New Reminder** in the bottom corner. Give it a name, then tap **Done**.

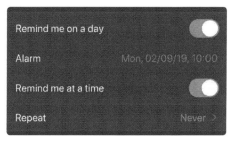

Remind yourself at a date and time

To remind yourself to do something at a specific date and time, tap on the new reminder, then tap the **i** button. On the next panel, tap **Remind me on a day**, then set a day and specific time if necessary.

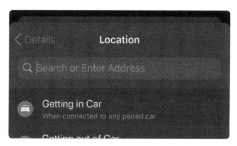

Remind yourself at a location

Similarly, you can also remind yourself when you reach a location. To do this tap the **Remind me at a location** button, then either enter an address or choose from one of the suggested options.

Share a reminder with someone

To share a reminder with someone else, tap on the Reminder then tap the **options** button in the top-right corner. In the pop-up panel, you'll see an option to invite people from your Contacts book.

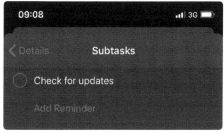

Create a subtask

You can add a subtask to more complex reminders or lists. To do this tap on the reminder, tap the **i** button, then scroll down and choose **Subtasks**. Tap on it and then hit **Add Reminder** to add a subtask

Create a group of reminders

From the home screen of the Reminders app, tap **Edit** in the top corner then hit **Add Group**. Give the group a name then tap **Create**. You can now drag and drop reminders into this group to categorize them.

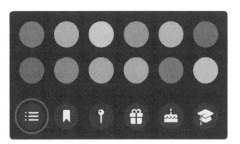

Assign a color and icon

From the home screen of the Reminders app, slide a reminder towards the left then tap the **info** button. In the pop-up window, you'll be able to re-name the reminder, assign a color and give it a unique icon.

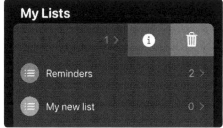

Delete reminders

From the home screen of the Reminders app, slide a reminder towards the left then tap the red **trash** icon to delete it. You can delete multiple lists and reminders by tapping **Edit** in the top-right corner.

Create a reminder using Siri

You can also add reminders by using Siri. Just hold the **Power** button, then say something like "*Remind me to pick up Sam*". Siri will then automatically create a new reminder.

153

Maps, News, and Utilities

Create your own Siri Shortcuts

Create complex actions then perform them using just your voice...

Think of Siri Shortcuts as an app that lets you create complex tasks and actions, then invoke them by asking Siri. So, you can do things like ask Siri "where's my next appointment" and the digital assistant will give you instant directions to the next event in your calendar. Similarly, you might say "turn today's photos into a collage", and Siri will automatically grab any photos from the day and turn them into a beautiful collage.
To find the Siri Shortcuts app, ask Siri to open it or look for this icon on the Home Screen:

The basics of using Reminders

1. Tap **Edit** to delete or duplicate shortcuts.

3. Access your existing shortcuts here. You can also **tap and hold** on a shortcut to rename it, duplicate it, see more details or delete it.

5. To discover a massive amount of Siri shortcuts tap the **Gallery** button then take a look around. You'll discover shortcuts based around accessibility, the home, daily routines and much more.

2. Tap the **plus** button to quickly create a brand new shortcut.

4. Tap the **Automation** button at the bottom of the screen to create an action that automatically runs at a certain time, place, event, or setting change.

Chapter 6

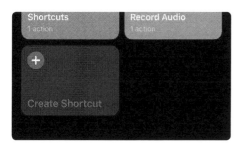

Create a new shortcut

Let's create a new Siri shortcut that instantly opens Safari then goes to the Apple homepage. Start by tapping the **New Shortcut** button.

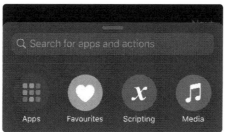

Add an Action

In the New Shortcut screen, tap **Add Action**. You'll see a selection of suggested actions and shortcuts fill the screen. Tap the first one, called **Apps**.

App actions

Look for **Safari** and tap it. Scroll through the list of Safari actions until you see **Open URLs**, then tap it.

Enter an URL

Tap on the faint blue URL text, then enter "www.apple.com".

Give the shortcut a Siri name

Tap **Next**, then type a name for you to call when you invoke Siri. In this example, let's call it "Open The Apple Website". Tap **Done** when you're finished.

Invoke your new shortcut

You're now ready to test your new shortcut. Hold down the **power** button to access Siri, then say out loud "open the Apple website". With a bit of luck, Safari should instantly open and take you to Apple's site.

Add a shortcut to the Home Screen

From the Siri Shortcuts home screen, **tap and hold** on a shortcut then tap the **Details** button. On the following screen tap **Add to Home Screen** double check everything looks good then tap **Add**.

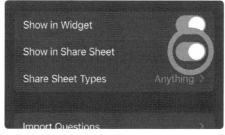

Add a Shortcut to the Share Sheet

If you'd like to regularly invoke a Shortcut then adding it to the Share Sheet is a good idea. To do this **tap and hold** on a shortcut then tap the **Details** button. On the following screen toggle **Show in Share Sheet**.

Select a specific Wi-Fi network

Here's an example of another Siri Shortcut: to select a specific Wi-Fi network when you go somewhere, tap on **Automation** > **Create Personal Automation** > **Wi-Fi**, tap on **Network** then choose your preferred Wi-Fi connection.

Maps, News, and Utilities

Create, edit, and share Notes

Learn how to quickly jot down notes, plus much more...

On first glance, the Notes app is a fairly basic way to jot down ideas and lists. It's much more than that, however. With the Notes app you can collaborate with friends, draw and annotate, scan documents, format text, create grids and more.

To find the Notes app, just look for this icon on the home screen of your iPhone...

The basics of using Notes

1 Collaborate and share a note with someone else by tapping this icon.

2 Share, print, or save a note by tapping the **Share** button.

3 Format text with headings, style, or layouts by tapping the **Aa** button.

4 Create a checklist of items by tapping the **tick** icon.

5 Add a scaned document, photo, or sketch, by tapping the **plus** button.

6 Create a table within a note by tapping this icon.

7 Add a sketch or drawing by tapping this button.

156

Chapter 6

Create a new note

To create a new Note, open the **Notes** app then tap the **New Note** button in the bottom-right corner.

Sketch a note

If you'd like to draw into a note, tap the **plus** icon or **pencil** button. A sketchpad will now appear on-screen, enabling you to draw with a pen, felt tip or pencil.

Change the line color

You can change the color of the line by tapping the small black circle. Tap the color wheel to access even more colors.

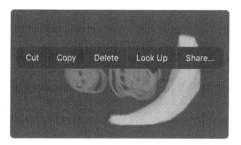

Delete a drawing

To quickly remove a sketch tap and hold on it then choose **Delete** from the pop-up field.

View thumbnails of your notes

If you'd rather see thumbnail images of each note, rather than a list, go to the home page of the Notes app, pull it down, then tap the **thumbnail** button.

Insert a photo

To add a photo to a note just tap the **camera** icon above the keyboard, select **Photo Library,** then choose the relevant image.

Create a table

If you want to create a simple, beautiful grid, then it's easy with Notes. Start by creating or opening a note, tap where you want to insert the table then tap the **table** icon just above the keyboard. You'll then see a 2-by-2 table appear within the note.

You can add content to a row or column by tapping the appropriate area, or add additional rows and columns by tapping the buttons above or to the left of the table.

To copy, share, or delete a table, tap anywhere within the table itself, then tap the **table** icon above the keyboard. In the pop-up window simply choose the relevant option.

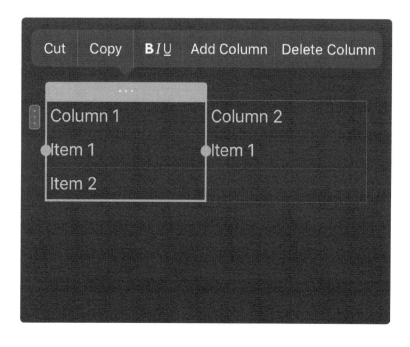

Create, edit, and share Notes

Share a note

Want to send a note to someone else? Just tap the **Share** button and you'll see options for emailing the note, sending it to another device via AirDrop, or copying it.

Print a note

While viewing a note, tap the **Share** button, scroll down then select **Print**. Please note that the iPhone can only print to wireless printers connected to the same Wi-Fi network.

Delete a note

While viewing the notes list just swipe across the note you wish to remove from right to left. Alternatively, you can tap the **trash** icon while editing a note.

Collaborate on a note

If you'd like to share and collaborate on a note with friends and family then it's an easy process on iPhone. If you're the creator of the note then it's yours to share, meaning you can invite others, see changes happen in real-time, and remove anyone at any time. Here's how it works:

Select the note that you would like to share, then tap the **Collaborate** button at the top of the screen (it's next to the Trash icon).

Use the Share panel to invite others from your Contacts book. You can also send invites via Message, Mail, Twitter and more.

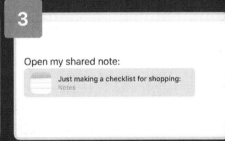

Anyone invited will receive an iCloud link to open your note. If they're using iOS then they can simply tap the link to open the note immediately.

As they make changes to the note you'll see them appear in real-time with a yellow highlight that fades away after a moment.

To remove someone's permission, tap the **Collaborate** button, tap the person's name then choose **Remove Access**.

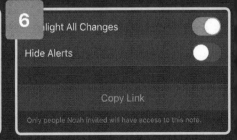

If you're tired of seeing notifications everytime someone makes a change, tap the **Collaborate** then un-toggle **Highlight All Changes**.

Chapter 6

Search for a note

To find a specific note, go to the home screen of the app, then pull down the notes list using your finger. You'll see a search field slide down from the top of the screen.

Add a grid background to notes

You can add a variety of grid-based backgrounds to your notes. To do this tap the **share** button, scroll down, select **Lines & Grids**, then choose a style.

Change the default Notes account

The default notes account is used whenever you create a new note. If for any reason you need to change it, go to **Settings > Notes**, then tap the **Default Account** option.

Scan a document

Using the notes app, it's possible to scan letters and documents, then attach them directly to a note. What's great is that scans actually look like scanned documents, thanks to some clever post-processing which straightens the image and fixes any white balance issues. To scan a document:

While viewing a note, tap the **camera** icon above the keyboard.

Select the **Scan Documents** option.

When the camera view appears, move it over the document you wish to scan and your iPhone will automatically recognize it.

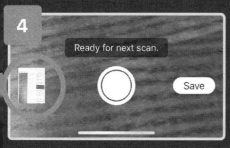

Tap **Keep Scan** to save the image. You can continue to scan further documents, or tap **Save** to attach the image/s to your notes.

The scan will now be attached to your note as an image.

Maps, News, and Utilities

Manage your Files

Discover how to manage files stored on your iPhone and within Cloud...

If you've ever used a desktop computer or laptop, then you'll feel at home using the Files app. It's basically a Finder app for the iPhone, letting you organize, edit and delete files across all of your Apple devices and cloud services. You can find the Files app by searching for it using Spotlight, or by looking for this icon:

Open the Files app and you'll see the Browse screen, with shortcuts to search through your files, browse iCloud Drive, see local files on your iPhone, and access any cloud-based services you have, such as Dropbox.

Files open or work in different ways depending on their file type. For example, images can be previewed, edited and marked up from within the Files app, while zip files can be previewed, but you can't extract their contents.

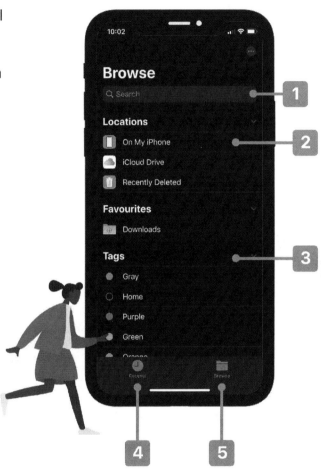

The basics of using Files

1 Search for a file on your iPhone or within iCloud using this search field.

3 If you've tagged any files with a color, then you can quickly find them by using these tag shortcuts.

5 If you're in the Recents view, then you can get back to Browse view by tapping this shortcut.

2 Quickly jump between files on your iPhone, within iCloud, or browse your recently deleted files.

4 See any recent files you've saved or modified by tapping the **Recents** shortcut.

Chapter 6

Swap to List View

If you want to fit more things onto the screen, tap the **List view** button in the upper-right corner of the screen. If you don't see it, pull the screen down with your finger.

Sort by size, date and name

While viewing a folder, tap the **Sorted by Name** drop-down near the upper-center of the screen to sort your files by name, date, size, or tag color.

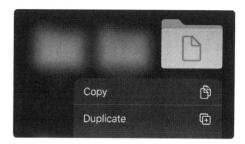

Tap and hold for more options

You can **tap and hold** on both folders and files to copy/duplicate/delete them, see more info, add a tag, favorite them and even compress/uncompress them.

See file information

If you want to see information about a file, such as its modified date or size and file type, **tap and hold** on the file until it lifts off the screen, let go then tap **Info** in the pop-up window.

Create a folder

Creating a new folder to organize your files is easy, just pull the window down, tap the options button, then hit the **New Folder** button.

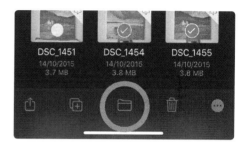

Move a file into a folder

Tap the **Select** button at the top of the screen, select the file/s that you want to move, then tap the **folder** icon at the bottom of the screen.

Drag and drop

One of the best features of the Files app is the ability to drag and drop files and folders. It makes organizing your files a breeze, lets you move multiple files at once, and tag files using a swipe. To get started, **tap and hold** on a file until it attaches to your finger. You can drag this file to another location, into a folder, or slide it over a colored tag.

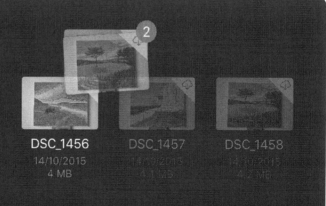

You can also drag multiple files at once using Multi-Touch. To do this, **tap and hold on the first file**, then use one of your other fingers to tap on another file. You'll see it attach to the stack under your finger. You can keep doing this to add as many files as you like, then drag them to where they need to be and let go.

Settings & Troubleshooting

Open the Settings app, and you'll find a wealth of options for customizing your iPhone. It's possible to configure Notification Center, add security features, change screen settings, and much more.

The Settings app is also an important tool for customizing accessibility tools, enabling those with visual impairments to read small text or adjust the color output of the display to counter for color blindness.

This chapter will cover all of the above, plus how to manage your iPhone's battery life, limit screen time, and much more...

Contents:

An overview of the Settings app	164
Use Screen Time to set limits	166
How to look after your battery	168
How to use Do Not Disturb	170
A guide to Accessibility settings	172
Audio Settings	176

Settings & Troubleshooting

An overview of the Settings app

Get to know the basics of Settings...

Whenever you want to make a change to your iPhone, adjust a setting, or update the operating system, then the Settings app is the place to go.

You can easily find the Settings app by looking for the icon with a cog gear in the center:

Open the Settings app and you'll see a list of shortcuts to all the important settings on your iPhone. They're labelled logically, so if you want to adjust how apps notify you, then tap on the Notifications shortcut. Similarly, if you want to connect to a new Wi-Fi network, tap Wi-Fi.

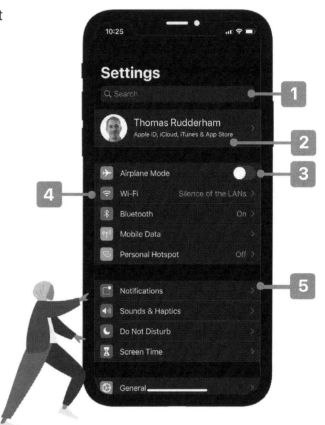

The basics of using Settings

1 Pull the Settings window down to access the Search bar.

3 Enable Airplane mode from here if you're boarding an aircraft, or need to save battery.

5 Configure notifications from this shortcut. Other shortcuts from the Settings homescreen include accessibility settings, Siri settings, and more.

2 Tap on your profile to access your Apple ID, where you can modify iCloud, iTunes, and device settings.

4 Access Wi-Fi settings, connect to a new network, or remove existing Wi-Fi settings from here.

164

Chapter 7

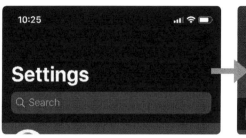  

Search through Settings

The Settings app is packed with toggle switches, fields, and features for customizing how your iPhone works. Many are hidden away in sub-sections that you probably wouldn't find unless you were really determined, so if you need to quickly change a setting, open the **Settings** app and drag the screen down. A search bar will appear, enabling you to quickly find a setting or switch.

Find individual app settings

To access individual app settings, open **Settings** then scroll down. Keep going and you'll find individual app settings. You can also search for an app by using the search box.

Prevent apps from running in the background

If you're worried that an app is running in the background and using up battery, go to its Settings panel, then toggle **Background App Refresh** off.

Prevent an app from tracking your location

From the same Settings panel, you can also prevent an app from tracking your location. You can choose to let an app track you all the time, when it's open, or never.

Check for system updates

If you'd like to check for the latest system update, go to **Settings** > **General** > **Software Update**. If an update is available, tap on it, enter your passcode, then set a schedule or update straight away.

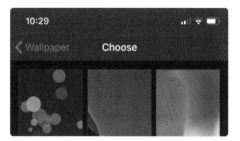 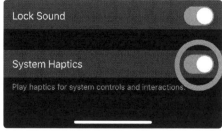

Choose a new wallpaper

Changing the background wallpaper is always a great way to freshen the look and feel of your device. It's easy to do, just open the **Settings** app, tap **Wallpaper,** then **Choose a New Wallpaper**.

Turn off System Haptics

Every now and then your iPhone will make a subtle vibration to let you know something has happened. If you don't like these effects, you can disable them by going to **Settings > Sounds & Haptics**, then toggling **System Haptics** off.

Update your Apple ID

Open the **Settings** app and tap on your **profile photo** to update and access all of your Apple ID settings. You can also manage your other devices and subscriptions from here.

165

Settings & Troubleshooting

Use Screen Time to set limits

Discover how much time you've spent using your phone, and limit future distractions...

If you're concerned or worried that you might be spending too long using your iPhone, then the Screen Time panel included in the Settings app will help you work out exactly how long you've spent using apps, how many notifications you've received, or set time limits to prevent future distractions.

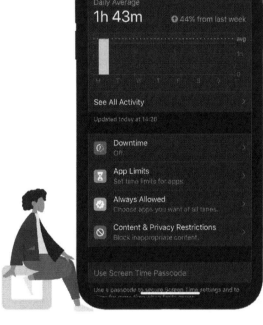

Find Screen Time

1. Open the **Settings** app, then tap on **Screen Time**.

2. Tap on your iPhone at the top of the panel.

3. You can then view your Screen Time data for the current day or the last 7 days.

As you'll see, the Screen Time panel is dense with information. You'll see total time spent with apps (some will be grouped into categories, such as "Productivity"), how many times you've picked up your iPhone, and how many notifications you've received.

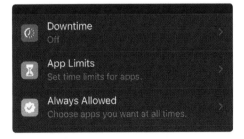

Downtime

Using the Screen Time settings panel it's possible to limit apps and notifications at a specific time, such as bedtime.

Set a Downtime schedule

Open the **Settings** app, tap on **Screen Time**, then choose **Downtime**. Toggle Downtime **on**, then use the From and To buttons to set a schedule.

Block inappropriate content

If you would like to limit inappropriate content, such as R-rated films or adult websites, tap on **Content & Privacy Restrictions**, then toggle it on. On the following screen you'll find a massive number of restriction options.

Chapter 7

View an activity report of your iPhone usage

Using the Screen Time panel it's possible to view daily or weekly reports of your iPhone usage. You can see how long you've spent using apps, how many notifications you've received, and even how many times you've picked up your iPhone.

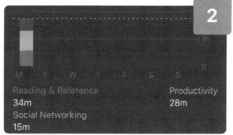

Open the **Settings** app, then tap on **Screen Time.** At the top of the panel you should see a brief report on your iPhone usage. Tap on it to see more details...

On the following panel you'll see a brief overview of the total time spent on your device, broken down into categories.

Beneath is a panel called Most Used. It displays which apps you've used the most during the day or last week. Tap on an app and you'll see a bar chart breakdown.

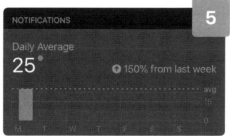

Below the Most Use panel is the Pickups panel. It displays exactly how many times you've picked up your iPhone, as well as the average amount of time passed between each pickup.

Further below is report panel of the notifications you've received. It's broken down by app, so you can see exactly which app is sending you the most notifications.

Other things you can restrict using Screen Time

By visiting the **Content & Privacy** panel in the Screen Time settings, you can limit a massive amount of content and features on a device, including:

- App installation
- Location Sharing
- Changes to passcodes
- Account changes
- Mobile data limits

- Volume limit
- Explicit language
- Screen recording
- Multiplayer games
- Explicit entertainment and books

167

Settings & Troubleshooting

How to look after your battery

Learn how to manage your iPhone's battery and more...

You might not know it, but batteries don't last forever. That's because every time you re-charge your iPhone, a tiny fraction of its battery capacity is lost. This means that if you re-charge your device every night, after a year it might lose approximately 10% of its original capacity.

The latest iPhone's do a pretty good at alleviating this problem thanks to some clever battery management techniques, but nevertheless, over time they will degrade to a small extend. Here's how you can see how your battery us faring, and what to do if it has degraded more than you were expecting...

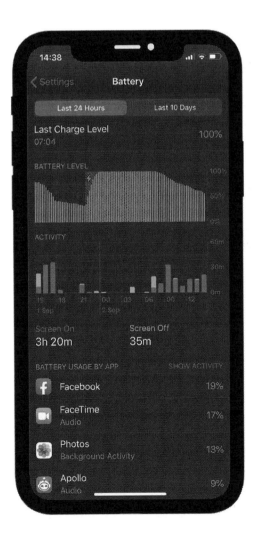

See your battery level over the last day

If you're worried that an app or service is using all your battery, then you can access a time chart which displays the battery level and activity over the last 24 hours, or 10 days. To do this:

1. Open the **Settings** app, then tap on **Battery**.

2. Scroll down and you'll find two charts covering your batteries charge level and activity.

3. You can toggle between the last 24 hours or 10 days using the blue tab above the charts.

4. Scroll down and you'll see a breakdown of which apps have used the most battery. Tap on one and you'll see the exact amount of time each app was used, and for how long it has been running in the background.

Enable Low Power Mode

If you'd like to extend your iPhone's battery for as long as possible, then iOS offers a handy mode whereby background activity, such as downloads and mail fetch, are switched off. The screen brightness is also reduced, and push notifications are checked less often. To enable Low Power Mode, go to **Settings > Battery**, then toggle **Low Power Mode** on. You can also enable or disable it from Control Center. Just look for the battery icon on there.

Chapter 7

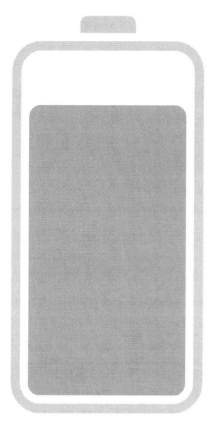

Battery Performance Management

If the battery has lost some of its original capacity, then Performance Management mode will be enabled and you will see this message:

This iPhone has experienced an unexpected shutdown because the battery was unable to deliver the necessary peak power. Performance management has been applied to help prevent this from happening again.

Performance Management works by throttling the CPU of your iPhone to prevent it from shutting down unexpectedly. This can sometimes happen when you do a CPU-intensive task (such as gaming). To turn this off, tap the **Disable** button. Please note that if you disable performance management, you can't turn it back on. Instead, it will be turned on again automatically if an unexpected shutdown occurs. The option to disable it again will then reappear.

See the total capacity of your battery

Over time your iPhone's battery will lose some of its total capacity. You can see where it currently stands by going to **Settings** > **Battery** > **Battery Health**. On the following screen you'll see its maximum capacity, relative to how it was when you first purchased the device.

If the total capacity is less than 80%

Chances are you've had your device a long time. Either that or you've re-charged it many many times. You're best option is to get the battery replaced by Apple. You can do this by sending it in for repair, by making an appointment at an Apple Store, or by visiting an authorized Apple Service Location.

To schedule a collection of your device, or to make an appointment with your local Apple Store, visit this URL: goo.gl/C4bHS1 It will take you Apple's website where you can select your device and arrange for the battery swap.

169

Settings & Troubleshooting

How to use Do Not Disturb

Prevent or limit interruptions and calls...

It can be rather annoying when a message, FaceTime call or notification awakes you at night, or when your device lights up and emits a noise during an important meeting. These notifications can usually be overridden by simply muting your device or putting it into Airplane mode, but the Do Not Disturb feature is simpler and much more effective.

It works by completely silencing your iPhone between a determined period of time, for example, midnight and 7 AM. During this time, your device won't make a noise, light up or vibrate. You can, however, tell it to allow notifications and calls to still come through from specified contacts.

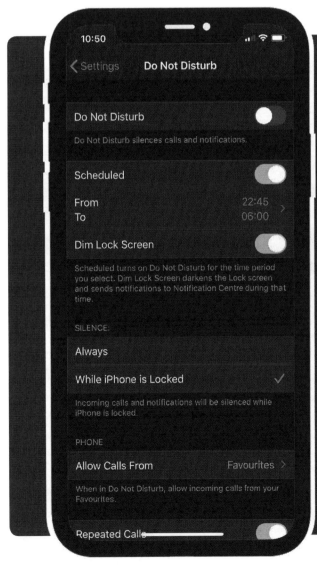

Exploring the Do Not Disturb panel...

To activate or schedule Do Not Disturb, go to **Settings > Do Not Disturb**, then toggle it **on**. You can then...

- **Schedule Do Not Disturb.** Use the **From** and **To** buttons to schedule Do Not Disturb, for example, when you go to bed.

- **Enable important contacts.** If you're expecting an important call, or need to let certain contacts get in touch at all hours, then tap the **Allow Calls From** button. On the next panel you can let anyone call, no one at all, or those in your Favorites list (created within the Contacts app).

Chapter 7

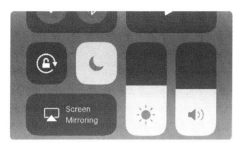  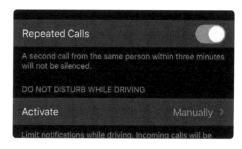

Enable Do Not Disturb

Swipe down from the top-right corner of the screen to access Control Center, then tap the button near the top that looks like a crescent moon. This will instantly enable Do Not Disturb, preventing any calls, messages or notifications from alerting you.

Activate for just a period of time

To quickly activate Do Not Disturb for the next hour, until the morning, or until you leave your current location, tap and hold on the **Do Not Disturb** icon in Control Center, then select an option.

Let repeat calls through

Toggle **Repeated Calls** on to let anyone bypass Do Not Disturb if they call more than once in a three-minute period. This might be helpful in emergency situations, or if there's something really important you should know about.

Configure Do Not Disturb while driving

Whenever you're driving, Do Not Disturb will prevent any calls, messages, or notifications from distracting you. It's a clever feature that's intended to make your journey safer, and it's fully customizable...

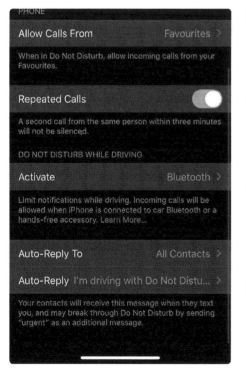

- **To access the Do Not Disturb While Driving panel**
  Go to **Settings > Do Not Disturb**, then scroll all the way down. At the bottom of the screen you'll see options for customizing Do Not Disturb While Driving.

- **Change how Do Not Disturb While Driving activates**
  Tap on the **Activate** panel to choose whether Do Not Disturb While Driving begins automatically, manually, or when your iPhone connects to a car's Bluetooth.

- **Send an Auto-Reply while driving**
  If someone tries to get in touch while you're driving, you can let them know via a text message by tapping on the **Auto-Reply To** button. On the following screen you can auto-reply to recent contacts, your favorites, or everyone in your Contacts book.

- **Change the Auto-Reply message**
  By tapping on the Auto-Reply button you can customize what the Auto-Reply message says. By default the message says: *"I'm driving with Do Not Disturb While Driving turned on. I'll see your message when I arrive at my destination."*

Settings & Troubleshooting

A guide to Accessibility settings

Enable visual, audio, and physical accommodations...

Your iPhone might be an intuitive device to use, but it's also packed with assistive features to help those with visual impairments or motor control limitations. You'll find the majority of them in the Accessibility panel within the Settings app. To get there, open **Settings** then select **Accessibility**.

Invert the colors of your screen

To flip the colors of your iPhone's screen, go to **Settings > Accessibility > Display & Text Size**. Scroll down and you'll see two options: Smart Invert, and Classic Invert. Smart Invert will reverse the color of everything except images, media and a limited number of apps. Classic Invert will reverse the color of everything on the screen.

Enable button shapes

Buttons in iOS usually look like a word or short piece of text. To make it more obvious which is a button and which is a piece of information, go to **Settings > Accessibility > Display & Text Size**, then toggle the **Button Shapes** switch **on**. This will display thin blue lines beneath buttons, and add small radio buttons to the inside of toggle switches.

Bold text

A handy accessibility feature for those with vision impairments is the Bold Text toggle switch. Once activated, it makes text on the display appear to be bolder. To turn on Bold Text, go to **Settings > Display & Brightness**, then toggle **Bold Text on**. Note that when this switch is toggled your iPhone will need to be restarted.

Show subtitles & closed captions

To enable subtitles and captions for entertainment on your iPhone, go to **Settings > Accessibility > Subtitles & Captioning**, and toggle the top switch **on**.

Style subtitles and captions

After enabling subtitles, tap the **Style** button to choose from three preset styles. By tapping **Create New Style** you can customize the font, size, color, and background style.

Use the LED flash for alerts

LED flash for alerts works by briefly flashing the LED on the back of the iPhone when a call or notification arrives. To enable this feature, go to **Settings > Accessibility > Audio/Visual** then toggle **LED Flash for Alerts on**.

Chapter 7

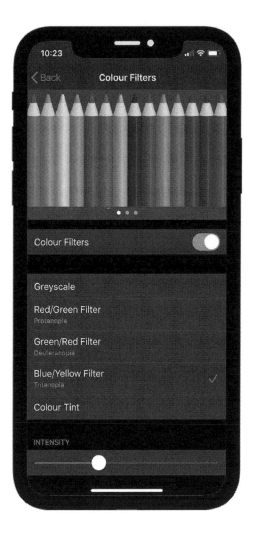

Adjust the color tint of the display to accommodate for color blindness

Color blindness can be a hassle at the best of times in the real world, and it's a problem that remains when using your iPhone to browse the web, examine photographs or generally interact with the user interface.

Thankfully a built-in accessibility feature can adjust the color palette of the display to accommodate for color blindness, making it possible to see tricky colors in a wide range of spectrums. Here's how it works:

1. Open the Settings app and go to **Accessibility** > **Display & Text Size** > **Color Filters** then toggle **Color Filters** on.

2. You'll see a preview of the effect in the graphic at the top of the screen (scroll it left to see two color charts).

3. To fine tune the color spectrum change, tap the filters below the image.

4. You can adjust the intensity of the effect using the slider at the bottom of the screen.

Connect a hearing aid to your iPhone

By connecting a hearing aid to your iPhone you can experience higher-quality phone conversations, FaceTime calls and more. Go to **Settings** > **Accessibility** > **Hearing Devices**, where you can connect to any Bluetooth-enabled hearing aids. Any hearing aids with HAC compatibility (visit support.apple.com/kb/HT4526 to see a list of compatible devices) will also enable you to increase and decrease the volume independently for both ears, monitor battery usage and more.

Change the audio balance

If you're hard of hearing in one ear, or have a faulty pair of headphones, then it's possible to adjust the volume level in either the left or right channels. Go to **Settings** > **Accessibility** > **Audio/Visual**, then scroll down until you see a slide with L on the left side, and R on the right. Drag it left or right to adjust the volume. It might help to play music via the Music app while you make the adjustment.

A guide to Accessibility settings

How to use Assistive Touch

Assistive Touch is a fantastic feature for those with impaired physical and motor skills. It enables you to activate Multi-Touch features such as pinch-to-zoom with only one finger. That's not all, it also enables you to trigger hardware features such as the volume buttons, and even rotate the screen or take a screenshot. It might sound complicated, but this feature is a doddle to use after a little practice.

To enable Assistive Touch, go to **Settings** > **Accessibility** > **Touch** > **Assistive Touch**, then toggle the button at the top of the screen.

You'll see a small square button appear on the side of the screen. By tapping this you can access a series of shortcut buttons which enable you to activate Notification Center, Control Center, Siri, functions on your iPhone, return to the Home screen, or quickly access your favorite gestures.

Create an Assistive Touch gesture

If you'd like to mimic a Multi-Touch gesture (such as zoom) using Assistive Touch, then it's possible to do this by using a custom gesture. To create one, go to the Assistive Touch panel in the Settings app, then tap the **Create New Gesture** button. On the following screen, use two fingers to mimic zooming out of an image. Once you've done, tap the **Save** button at the top of the screen. You can now use this gesture from the Assistive Touch panel by tapping the **Custom** button, indicated by a star.

How to use Speak Selection

Siri is great for setting reminders, opening apps or finding out what's on at the cinema, but you can also use Siri to read out loud selected text, messages, and notes.

This feature, called Speak Selection, is particularly useful for those with impaired eyesight, but it's also a fun way to playback text and messages using Siri's voice.

To turn on Speak Selection go to **Settings** > **Accessibility** > **Spoken Content**, then toggle **Speak Selection**.
To speak words out loud, highlight any text (by double-tapping or tapping and holding on it), then tap the **Speak** button in the pop-up menu. If you can't see the Speak button, tap the small right arrow on the pop-up menu and then choose **Speak**.

You can also read Emojis out-loud to make friends and family laugh. To do this just double-tap on the **Emoji** to select it, then ask your iPhone to speak the Emoji out-loud.

Chapter 7

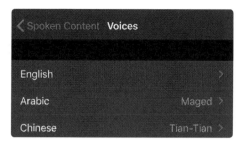  

Change the voice accent

You can choose from a wide range of voices from the Spoken Content menu. These include Australian accents, British accents, Spanish, Hindi and much more. You can also specifiy how fast your device reads text by dragging the **Speaking Rate** slider button.

Speak Screen

This helpful feature works by reading out-loud all the content that's currently on-screen. To enable Speak Screen, toggle its switch on from the **Speech** panel, then whenever you want to hear what's on-screen, swipe down from the top of the screen with two fingers. A panel will appear that enables you to control speech playback. To close the panel, simply tap the **X** button.

Highlight words

Notice the **Highlight Content** button? Toggle this switch to see the words highlighted as your iPhone reads them out-loud. Think of Karaoke and you'll get an idea of how this works.

Use an on-screen magnifying glass

The iPhone is designed to be easy for anyone to use, even those with visual impairments. However, there might be occasions where you need to zoom into the screen. Perhaps the text on a website is too small, or you can't quite make out the detail on an image. Those with visual impairments might also appreciate the ability to get a closer look at things on the screen. Using a three-fingered Multi-Touch gesture, it's possible to display an on-screen magnifying glass, which you can move around to examine things in more detail. Here's how to works:

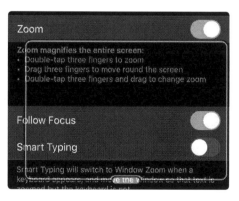

1. Go to **Settings** > **Accessibility**, then tap the **Zoom** option near the top of the screen.

2. You'll see a magnifying glass appear on-screen.

3. You can move the magnifying glass around by dragging the small button at the bottom of it.

4. You can hide the magnifying glass by tapping twice on the screen with three fingers.

175

Settings & Troubleshooting

Audio Settings

Personalize your iPhone to sound a little different...

A little personalization can go a long way towards making your iPhone feel like your own device. One of the easiest ways to do this is to alter the sound effects it emits. These include ringtones, email tones, tweet sound effects, calendar alerts, the lock sound, and keyboard clicks.

Over the next two pages, you'll learn how easy it is to select different tones and switch off sound effects that you might not need. You'll also discover how to set an automatic sound check feature, and set a volume limit.

Volume settings

Begin by going to **Settings** > **Sounds & Haptics**, where you'll see a large range of audio options appear on-screen. The slider near the top of the screen enables you to alter the volume level of all sound effects.

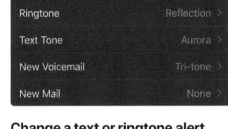

Change a text or ringtone alert

The buttons just below the volume slider enable you to choose from a wide variety of alert effects. Choose an option (such as **Text Tone**), then tap on a sound effect to preview and select it.

Download new tones

While selecting a new sound effect tone, tap the **Store** button to find new tones in the iTunes Store. Some are taken from popular music tracks, while others are custom sound effects purpose-built for your iPhone.

Disable/enable Lock Sounds

You can disable or enable the lock sound effect by toggling the **Lock Sounds** switch near the bottom of the screen.

Turn off keyboard clicks

Your iPhone will automatically emit a keyboard click sound every time you press a key on the on-screen keyboard. You can disable this by toggling the **Keyboard Clicks** switch at the bottom of the screen.

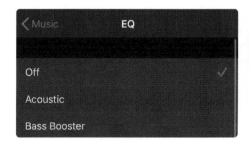

Change the music equalizer

Go to **Settings** > **Music** > **EQ**. On the following panel you'll be able to choose from a number of equalizer settings. Not all are self-explanatory, so try playing an audio track in the Music app while choosing from the different options.

Chapter 7

  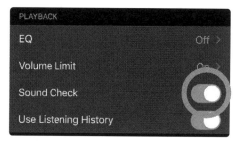

Set a volume limit

Over time our hearing becomes less sensitive, but it can also be damaged by listening to loud music for long periods of time.

To prevent hearing damage while listening to music on your iPhone, go to **Settings** > **Music**, tap the **Volume Limit** button, then lower the setting by dragging the slider button to the left.

This will prevent your device from playing music at a volume higher than what is selected.

Stream high-quality music over a cellular data connection

If you really appreciate high-quality audio while listening to music, and don't mind eating into your bandwidth allocation, then it's possible to stream uncompressed music when listening to Apple Music.

To do this go to **Settings** > **Music** > **Mobile Data**, then toggle **High Quality on Cellular**.

Enable Sound Check

This clever feature will automatically scan your music files, then set an automatic level that lowers and increases the volume to make tracks and albums sound more coherent across the board.

From the **Music** panel in **Settings**, toggle the **Sound Check** switch to enable this clever feature.

Troubleshooting

Most of us will never encounter a serious problem with our iPhone. However, every now and then something might go wrong. Perhaps the battery doesn't last as long as it used too, or maybe a glass of water is spilled over the device. This brief chapter will cover the most common problems, and also explain how to book and attend a Genius Bar appointment.

Contents:

The Genius Bar	180
AppleCare+	182
How to erase and restore an iPhone	183
What happens to a water damaged iPhone	184
Cracked Screen	185
What to do if you lose your iPhone	186
Other Problems	187

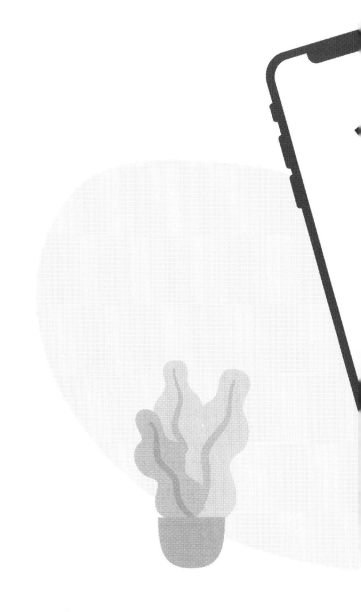

Settings & Troubleshooting

The Genius Bar

Get help when you need it most...

The Genius Bar is a technical support service in every Apple Store where you can get help to solve a problem or receive a replacement device.

They're often referred to as the heart and soul of an Apple Store. Every Genius Bar is manned by a team of technical specialists called "Geniuses". Each has experience solving a wide variety of hardware and software-related problems. They're also friendly and understanding to boot.

Are the team at the Genius Bar actually geniuses? Ask, and you're likely to receive a shrug, a wink, or a bemused look; but these dedicated guys and gals solve even the most complicated problems on a day-to-day basis. If they can't fix a problem with your iPhone then no one else can.

Most services at the Genius Bar are carried out for free. Repairs are carried out in the store, often while you wait. If the Genius can't repair the device on the spot, then a replacement is usually offered.

Chapter 7

Booking a Genius Bar appointment

The easiest way to book a Genius Bar appointment is via the Apple Store website. The URL changes depending on your location, but Google search "Book a Genius Bar appointment" and the first result should take you to the right page. From the website, you can select your nearest store and choose a suitable time and date – right down to the exact 10 minutes that suit your needs.

Please note that you'll need an Apple ID to book an appointment. This enables the Apple Genius to see your previous software and hardware purchases, which might prove to be helpful when diagnosing problems. It also makes paying for replacements and services much quicker.

Keep in mind that the Genius Bar is a popular service, so the first available appointment might be weeks in advance.

Attending the Genius Bar

Before going to the Genius Bar, make sure to fully backup your device. You can backup your iPhone via iCloud, or iTunes on a computer. Both methods save all your apps, text messages, photos, contacts, settings and more. These can be transferred to the new device once it's activated.

If you've never walked into an Apple Store then worry not. They're designed to be easy to understand and navigate. That is if the throngs of crowds aren't in your way. The front of the store is laid out with wooden tables with the most recent devices available to test and play with. Further back you'll see Macs and accessories, and on the back wall is the Genius Bar. If the store is configured in a different way (for example it has multiple rooms/halls), then look for the long wooden bench with black stools in front of it.

You check in with an employee holding a blue iPad. Can't see them through the crowd? Look for any other employee in a blue shirt, they'll be able to help. Alternatively, you can check in using the Apple Store app, but being met face-to-face is always more reassuring.

Once you're at the Genius Bar be polite and explain the problem with your device. The Genius team interview dozens of customers each day, sometimes hundreds. It's likely they've encountered every kind of problem, whether hardware or software related, and should be able to quickly identify what's wrong with a device. Research shows that a smile and positive attitude is the best way to get good customer service, and that applies to both employee and customer. Whereas creating a scene might get you thrown out of the store by security, a friendly chat could get you a free repair or additional advice.

AppleCare+

Work out if you need it or not…

AppleCare+ provides you with two years of repair or replacement coverage for your iPhone, iPad, or iPod touch. This includes two claims of accidental damage or failure of the battery to hold a charge of less than 50% of its original specification. You also get access to telephone technical support. Replacements aren't free, however. You'll need to pay an excess fee of $79, plus applicable tax. Nevertheless, it's still considerably cheaper than replacing the device without AppleCare+, which can cost up to $229.

Other benefits included with AppleCare+ include:

- Mail-in repair. A pre-paid box is posted to your address. Place the device in the box, send it for free and the device will be replaced or fixed.
- Carry-in repair. Take your iPhone into an Apple Store or other Apple Authorized Service Provider and it'll be fixed/replaced on-the-spot.
- Hardware coverage: AppleCare+ also covers the battery, earphones, USB cable and power adapter.

Is AppleCare+ worth it?

This depends from person to person. If you've ever dropped a mobile phone more than once then AppleCare+ might be a good idea. Similarly, if your household is shared by children or pets than you might want to look into buying technical support. Those who enjoy wild parties on a regular occasion might also want to buy the extra coverage. But if you're the sort who buys a case and keeps the device within reach at all times, then it's unlikely you'll ever need AppleCare+. Instead, it offers peace of mind and reassurance.

Chapter 7

How to erase and restore an iPhone via recovery mode

When only the worst has happened...

This is a bit drastic, so only perform a wipe and restore if the Apple logo has been stuck on-screen for more than 10 minutes. Here's how it's done:

1. Plug your iPhone into a Mac or PC with iTunes running.

2. Turn off your iPhone if it isn't already (you might need to force restart it).

3. Press and hold the **power** button for 3 seconds.

4. While holding down the **power** button, press and hold the **volume down** button, for between 5 and 10 seconds.

5. Let go of the power button but keep holding the **volume down** button for about 5 seconds (if you see the Plug into iTunes screen you've held it too long).

6. If the screen stays black then you've done it - your iPhone is now ready to restore using iTunes.

Settings & Troubleshooting

What happens to a water damaged iPhone

Try not to get it wet…

Water is usually a death sentence for electronic devices. That's because water conducts electricity, passing it instantly from one component to another causing them to overload. Impure water (such as fizzy drinks or sea water) also contains impurities that bind to electronics and corrode them. These impurities stay in the device even when it's dried, causing further damage over time.

Thankfully, the iPhone is water protected from liquids to an IP68 rating. That means you can drop your iPhone XR, XS or 11 into a liquid of two meters deep, for up to 30-minutes, and not see any damage to the internal components. The iPhone 11 Pro is protected in a liquid depth of up to 4 meters. If your iPhone sinks any deeper, or stays in liquid for a considerable amount of time, then you might be in trouble. Water damage typically causes the speakers and microphone to fail, can cause dark shadows to appear on the screen, or can break the device entirely. If you suspect this has happened, then it's a good idea to take your iPhone to the nearest Apple Genius Bar for repair or replacement.

It's worth noting that every iPhone and iPad includes a liquid damage indicator. This is a small strip inside the Lightning Bolt port that changes color on contact with water. The Genius uses this strip to detect the presence of water when identifying problems with a device. So if you've dropped your iPhone into very deep water there's little point pretending

Don't turn on a wet electronic device!

If you've accidentally dunked your iPhone into liquid then you're probably okay to keep using as normal. Just blow it dry and hope for the best. If it has been in liquid overnight, then do the opposite! Don't blow into it or shake the device, because if water has leaked into the casing this will only move it around and potentially cause further problems.

The best way to dry a wet iPhone

First of all, avoid any heat sources. Hairdryers are hot enough to melt the solder inside an iPhone. Similarly, avoid other heaters or sources of fire. Room temperature is your friend. The most efficient way to dry a wet device is to place it in a sealed container with silica gel packets. These are the same gels you find packaged with most large electrical devices. They typically come in small paper sachets.

If you don't have gel packets to hand, then white rice has been known to work. It's highly advisable to leave the device encased in rice for 24 hours, before repeating the process with a second portion of rice. Be patient, the longer you can leave the device to dry the more likely it will still work when it's turned back on. Good luck!

Chapter 7

Cracked Screen

Try not to panic!

If you've never dropped an iPhone then consider yourself lucky, for the sickening sound of glass and metal hitting a hard surface will make any stomach drop. It doesn't matter how strong a piece of glass is – it can, and will, break under certain conditions. Glass is particularly prone to knocks around edges and corners. On the iPhone it's common to see breaks emanate outwards from the lock/mute button.

iPhone uses Gorilla Glass for the construction of its screen. Gorilla Glass is created through a proprietary process that sees raw materials being blended into a glass composition that's microns thick. A chemical strengthening process then sees large ions being "stuffed" into the glass surface, before the glass is placed in a hot bath of molten salt at 400°. Needless to say, it's a complicated process that results in the strongest glass available in a consumer product. The process is refined and improved every few years, resulting in stronger versions of the glass that are subsequently manufactured into the latest devices. The most recent iPhones and iPads use Gorilla Glass 6, which is claimed to be 40% more scratch-resistant than earlier iterations.

Cracked screens are incredibly dangerous and should be fixed immediately. The fine cracks in Gorilla Glass will cut skin on contact, and it's possible that small pieces will fall out causing further problems. So, what's the best course of action when the glass screen on your iPhone is broken?

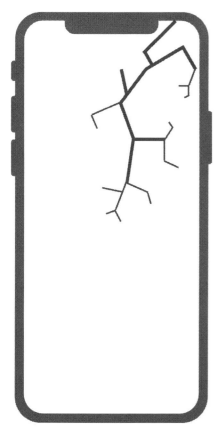

AppleCare+

If you've already purchased AppleCare+ then congratulations, because a replacement screen for your device will cost you an excess fee of $29, plus applicable tax. If you've already broken the screen and wish to buy AppleCare+ then you're out of luck..

Take your iPhone to an Apple Store

The price of replacing a screen differs from one iPhone to another. Older devices use separate components for the glass and LCD, whereas recent iPhones include composite screens that merge an OLED with the glass. This improves color reproduction and reduces glare, but increases repair costs. Here's a quick breakdown of the screen replacement costs:

- iPhone 6, iPhone SE: $129
- iPhone 8, iPhone 7, iPhone 6s, iPhone 6 Plus: $149
- iPhone 8 Plus, iPhone 7 Plus, iPhone 6s Plus: $169
- iPhone XR: $199
- iPhone X: $279
- iPhone XS: $279
- iPhone XS Max: $329

Settings & Troubleshooting

What to do if you lose your iPhone

First of all, don't panic!

It's probably somewhere obvious, like down the side of your sofa or in your jacket pocket. If you've looked around and still can't find it then there are a few things you can try...

Call it

Sounds obvious, right? Just use another iPhone or landline to call your iPhone and listen out for the ringtone.

Use your Apple Watch

If you're wearing your Apple Watch check to see if it's still connected to your iPhone. If it's not connected you'll see a small red iPhone icon at the top of the screen. If it is connected then your iPhone isn't far away. Next, swipe up from the bottom of your Apple Watch screen to access Control Centre, then tap the **iPhone Alert** icon (it looks like the iPhone with curved lines on either side). After a second or two, your iPhone will emit a loud noise.

Use Find My iPhone

Use another device or computer and go to www.icloud.com. Try to log in. If two-factor authentication is enabled and you're asked for a passcode, use your Mac or iPad to get the code and enter it. If you don't have another iOS device or Mac, it's time to call Apple for further help.

Once you're logged into iCloud click the **Find iPhone** icon, then wait for your devices to load. Next, click on your **iPhone** via the Map screen, or click the drop-down icon at the top of the screen and select it. In the pop-up panel, you'll be able to play a sound, erase your iPhone or place it into Lock Mode.

Track your iPhone in Lost Mode

If Lost Mode is enabled while your iPhone is turned on and Location Services were activated then you'll be able to immediately track its location via the map screen. If Location Services were disabled when you turned on Lost Mode, then it's temporarily turned on to help you track the device. If your iPhone was turned off completely, then Lost Mode will activate when it's next turned on and you'll be able to track it then.

Erase your iPhone

If the worst has happened and you don't think you'll be able to get your iPhone back, then you can securely erase its contents to prevent someone from accessing your data. When erased an activation lock is enabled and Find My iPhone is automatically turned on. This means if your iPhone is ever restored by someone else you can still track it and be assured that they can't unlock it without your Apple ID and password.

Other Problems

How to quit troublesome apps, or even force your iPhone to reboot...

It's rare, but sometimes hardware buttons stop responding or become stuck. Perhaps the Power button no longer clicks or the volume buttons stop working. If your device is less than a year old, or covered by AppleCare+, then a replacement is free. If older than a year expect to pay a replacement fee. Make an appointment with the Genius Bar to find out, or alternatively, try using the Assistive Touch accessibility feature (see Settings chapter for more information.) This enables you to trigger hardware buttons via touch-screen controls.

If your iPhone has completely frozen and refuses to respond to taps or hardware buttons, then there are three solutions you can attempt:

Force quit an app

If an app stops working, freezes or acts up, just swipe up from the bottom of the screen, then stop halfway to access the multitasking window. Next, slide the app which has crashed, up off the screen. This will force quit the app and remove it from the iPhone's temporary memory.

Reboot your iPhone

Sometimes your iPhone might stop responding to touch. This is very rare, but it does happen from time-to-time. It might be an app that causes the problem, or a conflict within the operating system. In these extreme cases you can force the device to restart. To do this hold both the **Power** button and the **volume down** button simultaneously for between five and 10 seconds. When the iPhone restarts you can let go.

Let the battery run dry

If the hardware buttons are stuck or broken, then simply let the battery run dry. Note that this might take up to 10 hours.

Settings & Troubleshooting

Thanks for Reading!

That's it for now...

So, you've come to the end of the book. Hopefully you've discovered a trick or two that will help you to really make the most of your iPhone.

If you would like to get in touch, have tips of your own, or have spotted a problem, please send an email via mail@tapguides.co.uk

iPhone Guide

Published by:
Tap Guides Ltd
Exeter, EX4 5EJ

ISBN: 9781798042830

Copyright © 2019 by Tap Guides Ltd

All rights reserved. No part of this publication may be reproduced, stored or transmitted in any form or by any means, electronic, mechanical, photocopying, recording, scanning, or otherwise without written permission from the publisher. It is illegal to copy this book, post it to a website, or distribute it by any other means without permission.

External content

Tap Guides has no responsibility for the persistence or accuracy of URLs for external or third-party Internet Websites referred to in this publication and does not guarantee that any content on such Websites is, or will remain, accurate or appropriate.

Designations

Designations used by companies to distinguish their products are often claimed as trademarks. All brand names and product names used in this book and on its cover are trade names, service marks, trademarks and registered trademarks of their respective owners. The publishers and the book are not associated with any product or vendor mentioned in this book. None of the companies referenced within the book have endorsed the book.

Credits

Humaaans Illustrations:
Pablo Stanley
https://www.humaaans.com

Apple Watch Icon:
Dale Humphries
https://www.flaticon.com/authors/dale-humphries

Chapter 7

Index A-R

Quickly find what you're looking for...

A

Accounts 64
  Add calendar events 65
  Add your email account 64
  Look for a password 65
AirDrop 71
  Enable AirDrop 71
  Share a file 71
AirPlay 78
  Mirror your iPhone display 79
  Stream to an Apple TV 78
AppleCare+ 182
Apple Pay 76
  Choose which card to use 77
  Remove a card 77
  See recent transactions 77
  Use Apple Pay in a store 77
  Use Apple Pay online 77
App Store 134
  Check for app updates 135
  Get support for an app 135
  How to install an app 135
  In-app purchases 135
  Review an app 135
  Subscribe to Apple Arcade 135

B

Battery 168
  Battery capacity 169
  Low Power Mode 168
  Performance Management 169

C

Camera app on iPhone 11 or 11 Pro 114
  Access additional controls 115
  Adjust the aperture 118
  Adjust the aspect ratio 121
  Camera filters 121
  Camera focus 115
  Camera timer 119
  Capture outside the frame 118
  Enable the camera grid 121
  Night Mode 116
  Panoramic photos 120
  Portrait photos 117
  Quickly record a video 115
  Slow motion video 118
  Swap camera modes 115
  Time-lapse videos 119
  Zoom even further 115
Camera app on iPhone X, XR & XS 106
  Burst mode 110
  Camera focus 107
  Camera timer 111
  Enable 4K video recording 109
  Live Photos 107
  Panoramic photos 112
  Shoot a video 109
  Slow motion video 109
  Swap camera modes 107
  Take a photo from the lock screen 107
  Take a portrait photo 108
  Time-lapse video 111
  Turn the flash on and off 107
Control Center 52
  Brightness 53
  Do Not Disturb 53
  Flashlight 53
  Music controls 53
  Network settings 53
  Orientation Lock 53
Cracked Screen 185

D

Data Roaming 72
Display 54
  Adjust the brightness 54
  Auto-Timer 54
  Record the screen 55
  Take a screenshot 55
  True Tone 54

E

Emergency SOS 75
  Emergency Contacts 75

F

Face ID 44
  Set up an alternative look 45
FaceTime 102
  Access additional controls 103
  Add stickers and filters 103
  Call from Contacts 103
  Delete your history 103
  Make a FaceTime call 103
  Replace your face with a Memoji 103
Files 160
  Create a folder 161
  Drag and drop 161
  Move a file into a folder 161
  See file information 161
  Sort by size, date and name 161
  Swap to List View 161
  Tap and hold for more options 161

G

Genius Bar 180
Gestures and Buttons 48
  Access Apple Pay 49
  Access Siri 49
  Force quit an app 48
  Jump between apps 49
  Multitasking Screen 48
  Power off 49
  Return Home 48
  Search 49

H

Handoff 74
Home Screen 47

Create a folder 47
Delete an app 47
Move apps 47

I

iCloud 51
  Find My iPhone 51
  iCloud Drive 51
iPhone
  iPhone 3G 12
  iPhone 3GS 12
  iPhone 4 13
  iPhone 4S 13
  iPhone 5 14
  iPhone 5S 14
  iPhone 6 15
  iPhone 6S 16
  iPhone 7 17
  iPhone 8 17
  iPhone X 18
  iPhone XR 22, 24, 32
  iPhone XS 20
  iPhone XS Max 20
iPhone 11 32
iPhone 11 Pro 24
  A13 Bionic 31
  Audio 31
  Battery Life 30
  Cameras 26
  Night Mode 28
  Portrait Mode 29
  Super Retina XDR Display 25
  Water Resistence 30

K

Keyboard 66
  Accents 67
  Cut, copy and paste 68, 70
  Predictive Text 66
  Slide to type 66
  Swipe to type 67
  Symbols 67

L

Lock Screen 46
  Control Center 46
  Menu Icons 47

Spotlight 46

M

Mail 96
  Attach a drawing 99
  Attach a file from iCloud 97
  Attach images and videos 97
  Automatically unsubscribe 99
  Format text 98
  Forward an email 99
  Mark an email as Unread 98
  Move or mark multiple emails 98
  Print an email 99
  Save a contact to your device 98
  Save a draft email 99
  Scan and attach a document 97
Maps 144
  Drop a pin 146
  Enjoy a flyover tour 146
  Look Around 145
  Navigate floors 146
  Report an issue with the map 147
  Search indoor maps 146
  Search Maps using Siri 146
  See a 3D map 145
  See Transit information 146
  Share a location 146
  Turn-by-turn navigation 147
Messages 86
  Add a camera effect 91
  Create your very own Memoji 88
  Delete a conversation 87
  Digital Touch 92
  Explore the App Drawer 87
  Hide alerts 95
  See when a message was sent 87
  Send a full-screen effect 94
  Send a message 87
  Send an Animoji 90
  Send an emoji 90
Music 136
  Add music to your Library 137
  Automatically download music 137
  Browse your offline music 137
  Create a Playlist 138
  Delete a track or album 138
  See the top charts 138
  Share your music 139
  Shuffle music 138
  Turn off Apple Music 138
  View music lyrics in realtime 137

N

News 148
  Add a news source 148
  Change the text size 149
  Check out Apple News+ 149
  Save a story 149
  See your reading history 149
Notes 156
  Add a grid background 159
  Collaborate on a note 158
  Create a table 157
  Delete a drawing 157
  Delete a note 158
  Insert a photo 157
  Print a note 158
  Scan a document 159
  Search for a note 159
  Share a note 158
  Sketch a note 157
  View thumbnails of notes 157
Notifications 60
  Clear your notifications 61
  Configure notifications 61

P

Personal Hotspots 72
Phone 100
  Add a photo to a contact 100
  Assign a custom ringtone to a contact 101
  Block numbers 101
  Dial a number using Siri 100
  Forward calls to another number 101
  Respond to calls with messages 101
  See your mobile data usage 101
  Turn off Data Roaming 100
  Turn off your caller ID 101
Photos 122
  Add a filter 127
  Add a name to a person 125
  Adjustment tools 127
  Create an album 130
  Crop an image 127
  Edit a memory video 124
  Edit Live Photos 129
  Fine tune an image 127
  Hide photos 130
  How to delete a photo 126
  How to share a photo or video 126
  People and Places 125

Index S-W

Quickly find what you're looking for...

Rotate or tilt a photo 127
Search through your photos 125
Select multiple images 126
Share an event 124
Swap between day, month and year views 123
The basics of editing a photo 126
Trim and edit videos 130
Watch a video of an event 124
Protection
  Cases 38
  Screen Protectors 38

R

Reminders 152
  Create a group of reminders 153
  Create a new Reminder 153
  Create a reminder using Siri 153
  Create a subtask 153
  Delete reminders 153
  Remind yourself at a date and time 153
  Remind yourself at a location 153
  Share a reminder with someone 153
Roaming chargers 72

S

Safari 82
  Adjust text size 84
  Apple Pay 84
  Block ads and junk 84
  Clear your web browsing history 85
  Enable Private Browsing 85
  Go back a page 83
  How to enter a website address 83
  How to search the internet 83
  iCloud tabs 84
  Save a webpage as a PDF 85
  Search a web page 84
  Search suggestions 83
  Share a page 85

Show the control panel 83
  Tabs 83
Settings 164
  Accessibility 172
    Assistive Touch 174
    Audio balance 173
    Bold text 172
    Button shapes 172
    Color tint 173
    Connect a hearing aid 173
    Invert colors 172
    LED flash 172
    Magnifying glass 175
    Speak Screen 175
    Speak Selection 174
    Subtitles and Closed Captions 172
    Voice accent 175
  App settings 165
  Audio 176
    Keyboard clicks 176
    Music equalizer 176
    Ringtone alerts 176
    Volume limit 177
    Volume settings 176
  Check for system updates 165
  Choose a new wallpaper 165
  Do Not Disturb 170
  Find individual app settings 165
  Prevent an app from tracking your location 165
  Prevent apps from running in the background 165
  Screen Time 166
    Block inappropriate content 166
    Downtime 166
    View an activity report 167
  Search through Settings 165
  Update your Apple ID 165
Setup
  Activate your iPhone 42
  How to insert a SIM card 42
  Quick Start Tool 43
Siri 62
  Dictate text 62

Speak to Siri 62
Siri Shortcuts 154
  Add a shortcut to the Home Screen 155
  Add a Shortcut to the Share Sheet 155
  Create a new shortcut 155
Spotlight 58
  Spotlight Widgets 59
Stocks 150
  Delete a stock 151
  Rearrange your stocks 151
  See an individual stock 151
  Stock news 151

T

Troubleshooting
  AppleCare+ 182
  Erase and restore an iPhone 183
  Force quit an app 187
  Reboot your iPhone 187
  What to do if you lose your iPhone 186
TV 140
  Access movie special features 141
  Download a film 141
  Watch HDR movies 141

W

Water Damage 184
Wi-Fi 50
  Public networks 50
  Share a Wi-Fi password 50
Wi-Fi calling 73